TONEE

By Robert Becker

TONEE

I met Tonee at work selling her a fine automobile.

"C'mon Bobbie, make it happen."

She was a good looking middle aged slim blonde, over dressed in her black business suit on that sticky July afternoon. I kept thinking she must have been stunning years back. She was funny and upbeat.

Tonee had moved to Massachusetts the year before to reconnect with and take care of her Mother after twenty years in L.A. She had a good job here in sales at a local TV station. She dropped names to my manager and got a very strong trade appraisal and sales price on her new CPO Audi.

Tonee made decent money, but her ex had messed her credit, so her Mother would be needed as a co sign. Tonee said that would be no problem. Her Mother had great credit but little income.

It took a few days to get them back. Tonee's mother, Jackie, had agoraphobia and rarely left the house. She came in with the same deep voice as her daughter. She liked her attention. We were both Leos with our Birthdays coming up soon just two days apart. Jackie said she would need a Birthday kiss from her Leo to sign the paperwork.

I smiled, shucked and ducked.

Tonee just needed to bring in some supporting documents and the deal was done.

At work the next day, a funny thing happened on the way to the toilet. Walking my way with a funky bounce was the kind of high cheeked gorgeous blonde I might have approached twenty years earlier.

"Hi Bobbie." She was talking to me.

"Do I know you?"

"It's me silly, Tonee."

The voice was familiar, but different. Tonee was having a very good day. She brushed her hand on my shoulder as she passed. I could smell her perfume.

"I'll see you tomorrow Sweetie."

Which Tonee would come for her car tomorrow? Wow.

I'd been thinking of opening my life again. I hadn't been on a first date in fifteen years. I was five years without a woman's touch. My fiance of ten years dumped me when my business blew up in spectacular fashion five years before. My financial and legal hassles were finally gone. I was broke, but free and ready to live again after such a long negative ride.

Tonee was looking interesting and good. Would I have the nerve to ask her out? I sat at home that night talking to my two pussycats about what to do. The two honkers didn't help very much.

My familiar Tonee arrived at high noon excited for her new ride. We sat in the car as I showed her features and functions. We were both nervous. The scent of her perfume sent me to word. I asked if she'd go to dinner with me.

"I'd love to." Her voice was husky and welcoming.

I was to meet Tonee at seven. The road to Jackie's house was pre Revolutionary War, convoluted and ill marked. Compulsively punctual, I was flustered as I backtracked three times. I called and finally found the 150 year old farmhouse overlooking the Connecticut Valley. There was a newer addition in the back of the house and a big newer barn beyond.

I was nervous, but Tonee gave me a welcoming hug as I walked into the sun room where her Mother sat watching Bonanza at volume ten. Jackie made some small talk which I barely responded to. I met the two cats, Chloe, an older Tom taken in as a stray and Ziggy, Tonee's Maine Coon from California who was so soft and loving. I could feel Jackie's eyes on my back as we departed.

Tonee was dressed casually in her jeans and white blouse. She had a talkative nature which well made up for my poor conversational skills. We drove in my old BMW as Tonee talked about her work and her boss who hated her and how nice it was that she had reconnected with her family after twenty years in California. She also told me how she fractured her left thigh in the shower ten years before and then broke the lower shin bone on the same leg later that year. I shuddered as it brought memories of the three times I had broken my right leg playing soccer in my youth.

We had wine with dinner. I heard about her torn childhood, her parents divorcing in Pennsylvania when she was three. Her Mother, who used to be drop dead gorgeous, had been wooed by Gil, a flamboyant married Jewish man who owned a shoe store, and promised her a wonderful life. Tonee's Father, Harold, won custody, which was so rare in those days. He later remarried Elinor, who Tonee despised. She spoke glowingly of her Father and her step father relaying stories as if they had happened yesterday. Tonee talked of her anguish as the two families fought over Tonee's visitation schedule and care.

As we shared a piece of apple pie, Tonee mentioned that her best friend, Ellen, had died that morning in California of ALS. I was surprised Tonee was out with me tonight. I took her hand and kissed it.

"I'm so sorry Tonee."

I don't think she had fully absorbed the death. I held her hand the rest of the night. She had a gentle touch. We had a final drink and I walked with my arm around her waist to the car across the street. I could feel the dip in her walk from her shorter left leg. Her stride was slow.

Sitting in the car, I reached over and kissed her soft, welcoming lips.

"Thank you." Her voice was dusty and loving.

I could feel myself changing as we kissed in the chilly air.

We made plans for the next weekend. I kissed her goodnight and waited till she entered her house. The door wouldn't open. The house was dark. Tonee searched her purse for keys, then looked underneath a planter outside. She banged on the door and rang the doorbell. She came back to the car and said I should leave, that she'd be okay. I walked her to the front of the house and she rang the front doorbell. I could hear the phone ringing as Tonee called. Ten minutes later, a light went on. Tonee's mother stood at the rear door with her walker and let her baby girl in.

The phone rang just as I entered my house.

"It's me, Tonee. I just wanted to make sure you were home okay."

Sweet girl.

Like an unstoppable invasion, the sight, the smell, the thought of Tonee rapidly overcame my defenses.

We dated a second time. We talked on the phone each day. I heard more and more stories of her childhood; of her Father who was adored and who cared for Tonee with intelligence and character; of Gil, her Jewish step dad whose influence was so compelling, Tonee converted to Judaism when she was sixteen, totally of her own initiative; of her Mother whose physical beauty was undeniable, who never worked a day in her life, but left her daughter with crippled self worth; and the step mom who had a special level of cruelty and indifference towards the fragile child in her care.

Beneath it all, was her full belief in the life of the soul, of the need and want to be good, of the belief in her lives lived and the afterlife. She had faint visions of her prior existence.

Tonee would describe events and youthful

times distant decades past with a freshness that lived in the spoken moment. Her memories of recent decades were often scattered or lost.

I so wanted to touch her, to feel her, to absorb and penetrate her soul and body. On our third date, after a good Vietnamese dinner, I boldly asked Tonee if she'd like to meet my pussycats.

"I'd love to."

The moon rose red and full. I could feel its energy. The rush of thoughts and lust focused in our silent drive to the old house on the hill where I lived. I helped Tonee out of the car and up the grassy slope to the porch stairs in the hundred year old Victorian.

"Wowzers Bobbie, nice place."

The big fat Brother pussycats rushed the door, grey Freddie and Pita white with grey spots, sniffing Tonee's feet. The light in the hallway showed the big living room with the grand fireplace. The floors were polished oak. I walked Tonee through to the dining room and into the kitchen which had wainscoating and a tin ceiling with a rain hole in the far corner. I hoped to show Tonee my bedroom later which was up the stairs off the entranceway. My landlord used the rest of the second floor, which was walled off, but he was rarely there, spending his time at his other house down the street.

Tonee admired my collection of ancient pottery from Israel. When she went to the bathroom, she asked me why the mirror was covered. My Father had died eleven months earlier. Jewish tradition called for covered mirrors for a year. Tonee asked if she could take down the cover, that what was most important was how you acted while the person was still alive. I took off the towel in the half bath at the bottom of the steps and from the full bathroom near the kitchen. It

6

felt strange and good. I had taken my Father's death in Israel harder than I had expected. We had our very bad times together, but had made peace long before his death.

I hugged Tonee and kissed her in the hallway.

"Thank you for coming."

I had been alone for years with my ten year old honkers. Tonee reached out to the pussycats. They were shy, but gave in to her touch.

I started with a nice Chateau Neuf De Pape and sat with Tonee on the couch to sip wine and touch lips. I tried not to be too forward. It had been a long time for me and I couldn't imagine misstepping with my beautiful woman. After a short time, I asked her if she'd like to go to the bedroom.

"Yes."

I called the pussycats and shut them off with the French doors in the middle room where they slept.

I knew Tonee had no ass. I had always been an ass man. To my surprise and delight, she revealed a remarkable set of breasts.

"Where have you girls been hiding?"

Tonee laughed. We lay in bed hugging. Tonee showed me her wonderful angel tattoo on her right shoulder blade. Her skin was soft and brilliant to my touch.

I entered her. She gasped and smiled, groaning and moaning as she came time after time for hours.

"Where have you been all my life?" She kept screaming.

I wouldn't cum for three hours, amazed at her need and the voice that kept asking for more.

"Where have you been?"

As I lay beside her in the deep night, she rose, that ephemeral nymph I had met once before, her changeling aura alive in the moonlight, passing down the stairs, to return with a plate of cheese and a bottle of wine, two honkers in her wake. I was amazed at the youth in her face and body. We sipped wine and lay down to sleep as dawn reached. The pussycats nestled with us, begging for cheese and attention.

"I love you Tonee."

"I love you Bobbie."

I curled behind her listening to quiet breath. Rubbing her head gently, I could feel jets of energy pulsing in tiny pathways. Slowly, the pulsing subsided, our bodies slipping to restful sleep, so beautifully worn and sore.

Reality cracked as I rose at 7 to prepare for work. Tonee was well into her deep sleep, not reacting to my gentle touch. I fed the cats, made coffee, scrambled eggs and toast to be served in bed. My walk was sore in a special way.

Tonee finally sat up and welcomed the coffee, barely nibbling at the eggs and toast.

I had something on my mind that I had dreaded to reveal. I told Tonee I had bad things to get off my chest. I told her about the collapse of my business and my inability to close it before more damage was done. I borrowed extra money from the bank under false statements because I was not strong enough to make the hard decision to close it. I ended up with three months in a half way house and three months electronic home detention, commuting to work at the dealership each day. That was five years ago. I had been through a severe depression. I finally paid off the debt with an advance that wiped out most of my inheritance. I had always had a very high level of

8

integrity and honesty. I was embarrassed and broke after 24 years of effort. Never in my craziest dreams, did I think I would be selling cars for my income at fifty two years old.

Tonee just looked at me and said "That's nothing. When I was at Pac Bell years ago, they sent me to a facility to straighten out. I was there for months for depression and substance abuse."

We hugged and made love. I called in sick to work. For the first time since we had met, we simply relaxed and talked. I told her about my family, my two religious brothers in Israel with their enormous number of children and my two brothers in Hawaii, the oldest a paranoid schizophrenic and my younger brother, a doctor in New Jersey. My parents were first cousins, marrying right after WW2. They always had a tumultuous relationship that damaged everyone. I told her there was a crazy brilliant edge in all of us, with the emphasis on crazy. I told her of my annual January vacation to Israel the last five years, since my parents had become ill. My Father died. My Mother had been sick with Parkinsons for years, her body and mind out of her control. I told Tonee I had been seriously thinking of moving to Israel or Hawaii, that I might be ready within the coming year.

"I always wanted a real brother or sister. I have two step sisters, but I always felt alone."

We kissed and made love. I felt the beginning of a long us.

"You know Tonee, the three great loves in my life have all been pretty crazy."

"I'll betcha I'm the craziest."

"I'll bet you're wrong." I had always favored beautiful intelligent women. Perhaps, I got bored if they didn't have enough twist.

Tonee called her Mother, going ashen with the conversation. We showered. I drove her home.

"Can I see you tonight?"

"Okay."

I could see her tension as she walked into Jackie's house. She had her list of shopping chores and laundry and cleaning up and the pressure of her Mother's constant demands.

I stopped at my favorite Italian deli and bought a hot capicolla sandwich to go. I watched the Red Sox on TV, sleeping into the late afternoon, looking forward to seeing my love again. I couldn't remember my last sick day from work. I didn't miss the place.

I waited till six to call my love. A deep voice answered.

"Hello."

"Hey Babe, I miss your touch badly. What time do you want me to pick you up?"

"Let me get my slut daughter to talk to you."

oops

"Hi Bobbie, I miss you."

"What time do you want to come over?"

"Oh no, not tonight Bobbie. I tired."

"You said you'd come over."

"No I didn't. I'm making dinner now for Mama. I still have laundry and finish shopping tomorrow. I work very hard Bobbie."

I was disappointed, but didn't want to argue.

"I love you Tonee."

"I love you Bobbie."

I had such a strange feeling in my body and my mind, stupid happiness. I felt joy. All I could consider was Tonee. I wanted to talk to her, to feel her, to smell her.

"I just feel good Tonee. And it's all your fault."

We talked each day. I would have to be careful when I called to be sure who was on the line. Sometimes, when her Mother answered, she did not let me know at first who I was talking to. Tonee also told me that her Mother sometimes picked up the other phone at home to listen.

I offered to cook dinner for Tonee. That made her happy. We agreed on Saturday night. Tonee would drive to my house for the first time after her day of chores. A good customer gave me a decent bottle of single malt Scotch, my old weakness. I picked up a big chicken and a few vegetables and was ready for my first home cooked dinner in years. I had always survived off the gas grill, but spiders had spun their webs inside my grill, and it wouldn't work well.

I started my one pot dinner, stuffing the chicken with bread and corn and cut up potatoes to simmer in the sauce. I put the oven on low and let the slow magic begin. I opened a Merlot and let it breathe. I took a neat sample of the Scotch to make sure Tonee would like it. Then I took another because it tasted so good.

I heard an Audi honk in the driveway. The neighbor's dogs barked. I raised the oven temperature to hasten the cooking and ensure the stuffing was fully done.

I met Tonee on the porch. She had a wonderful extra large smile. It felt great being with her again. She wore a blouse that actually displayed her beautiful girls.

"Wowzers Bobbie, what smells so good?"

"It's a secret. Would you like a shot of good Scotch?"

"Am I blonde?"

I put on some music. Tonee and I went

upstairs for a little re-acquaintance. We couldn't stay too long. I didn't want to ruin dinner.

The pussycats did a happy dance as I took the big pot out of the oven. The skin was crisp and the potatoes perfect. Tonee came to the kitchen without permission. She wanted a slice of breast meat.

"Wow Bobbie. How did you know I love corn?"

We had dinner while watching Food Channel, Tonee's favorite.

"You didn't tell me you're a great cook."

Tonee actually finished her plate. It was pretty good. I poured some wine. Tonee tried to play with the pussycats while I cleaned up. The Honkers followed the food, begging for scraps as I wrapped leftovers for the fridge.

This was a nice night. I tried to make the Scotch last, but Tonee kept giving me the don't be a cheapo look as I doled out shots slowly. Tonee wanted ice in her drink. Pita seemed to be taking to Tonee. Freddie had been scared a few years back when the apartment was broken into and went from being very outgoing to a big scaredy cat.

In bed, we lay in each other's arms, slow kissing with our mouths breathing together forever. I helped Tonee down the stairs to the bathroom as she almost fell.

"I'm okay Bobbie."

I lay behind her as her breathing slowed to sleep, feeling and rubbing the spots of energy in her beautiful head. I kissed the Angel on her shoulder, falling to a sleep of pleasant dreams. In the morning, I let Tonee sleep till she woke to the touch of a pussycat paw.

"I had some wild dreams last night Bobbie. I saw my Father and the schnauzers Gil used to have.

There was a great chase scene. It was fun Bobbie."

The plan was to have Tonee cook one of her great dinners for me at our house the following weekend. I couldn't stand the days absent from her presence.

Friday night, I was off work at five. Tonee arrived at my house about six thirty with bags of groceries and a few bottles that happy clinked as they were carried up the stairs. Tonee had rushed from work to shop for food and come right over. She had been rushing since six am. I could still smell cigarettes on her clothing. I asked if she wanted to shower, but she seemed anxious to make her meal. I hugged her and told her to relax. She reached into her bag and handed me a bottle of Scotch.
"This is for you Bobbie. Leave this girl alone in the kitchen."
"Do you want to light Shabbos Candles before you get busy?"
It wasn't dark yet, but Tonee said the prayers and lit the candles over the fireplace, covering her face with her hands.
"What did you wish for Bobbie?"

Tonee disappeared to the kitchen with the two fat cats falling in love with her preparation. I could hear clanking and cabinets opening and slamming shut and the refrigerator getting a rare workout. I heard the hissing of a frying pan and beautiful smells. I snuck a peak. Tonee was not a one pot cook. The kitchen was a mess. She had a glass with ice and clear liquid. She opened the freezer door and showed me her Absolut Vodka.
"Outta here Bobbie. Tonee rules."

Two hours from the start of preparation, Tonee's schnitzel was fabulous. She had smashed garlic potatoes and steamed broccoli, all smothered in butter. Tonee was a little weak on her feet. I offered to bring the plates of food.

"Outta my kitchen."

We ate in the dining room with the big picture of my parent's old relatives. I poured us some wine. Tonee finally sat down, exhausted, with a look of satisfied completion. Her food was wonderful. I love fried food. I ate too much. I told Tonee to relax. I would clean up. I asked if she wanted to shower.

"I'm too tired Bobbie. I rest."

I walked her to the couch and lay her down to sleep.

The kitchen was a nightmare. The stove and counters were layered in grease. She'd used numerous pots and dishes. I looked in the freezer. The Vodka was half gone. I took a little taste and finished the cleanup. I checked on Tonee. She had a little happy snore. I took another shower and sat down in my recliner to TV and Honkers.

After a couple of hours, I kissed her cheek as she slept. Her eyes opened, blinking,confused. In the sparse lighting all I could see were dark beads staring up at me.

"Are you Okay? Do you want to sleep upstairs? I'll help you."

Then I heard the voice, tight, different, so angry.

"I do not like you. There are so many ways on so many different levels I can imagine that I cannot trust you." Her eyes stared through me. "Just leave me alone."

I backed away. She rose, stumbling to the bathroom, then up the stairs in the dark to the bedroom. I felt like a player in the Twilight Zone. I sat down in my recliner and sipped Scotch with the pussycats on my lap and at my feet. I watched an old movie wondering what just happened to my newly wonderful life.

I had fallen asleep when I heard Tonee calling from upstairs.

"Bobbie, where are you Bobbie?"

I walked up to the bedroom, not understanding what was happening. I lay down in bed away from her. Tonee reached for me. I did not respond. She leaned over and kissed me. I did not respond. She smelt of sweat and alcohol.

"What's wrong with you Honey? Didn't you like dinner?" Her voice was young and light and playful.

"What do you expect from me? I don't understand what happened to you tonight."

"What do you mean? What's wrong Bobbie?"

"Don't you remember what you said downstairs earlier?"

"No, I'm sorry. What did I do?"

Tonee was shaking, holding me, looking as confused as I felt. I tried to explain what happened. She was very upset.

"I'm so sorry Robert. It's my fault. I've tried my best to keep you from my dark side."

"What do you mean?"

Tonee talked about her inner self and the demons that sometimes get out.

"I'm so sorry Robert. Can you forgive me?"

"I love you Tonee. I want to help any way I can. Just let me know when I make you angry. I want to understand."

"Hold me."

We loved slowly and gently before she rolled on her side to sleep. I spooned behind her with my lips on her Angel tattoo till I slept.

In the morning, I waited for Tonee to fully awaken. She seemed timid and scared, not wanting to talk. She went home by noon. We hugged before she left. I knew now I was in for something different.

The week went by in a normal way. Tonee complained about her job and her boss who hated her and her Mother who was Mama. Tonee told me she used the exaggerated pronunciation of Mama as a form of derision.

I was hating work and some of my sleazy coworkers. My vacation would come in January. I would visit Israel again while my Mother was still alive. I was seriously contemplating a move to Israel or Hawaii. I had talked to Tonee about this. She was less than a year back in Massachusetts with her family and was in no mood to move again in the near future.

We set up for Saturday after my work and her endless chores for Mama. Tonee described her Mama's coupon clipping and the places they went to save a nickel. Mama would wait in the car while Tonee went into the stores. I couldn't imagine all that walking with her bad leg.

I saw Tonee pull into my driveway. I rushed to help her with the grocery bags. She looked tired but wonderful.

"We went to eight stores today. Look what I got you." Tonee handed me a bottle of Scotch and kissed me.

"Would you like a taste Tonee?"

"Sure." She leaned over and kissed me.

Tonee disappeared into her kitchen. She was making stuffed peppers. I smelled the vegetables sauteeing from the living room. I sneaked in for a kiss, but she demanded her space. She had a drink working on the counter.

"What are you drinking tonight?"

Tonee opened the freezer door and showed me her Absolut vodka.

"Better for my tummy than the shit Vodka Mama drinks."

I brought the plates into the living room. Tonee lay down on the couch, exhausted. The dinner was delicious, but Tonee had not eaten. She looked so young and beautiful in her happy sleep.

I cleaned up the kitchen which wasn't as bad as the last time. I wrapped Tonee's dinner and put it in the fridge. After a couple more hours, I woke Tonee.

"Let me help you upstairs."

"I'm okay. How was dinner?"

Tonee stumbled to her feet and fell back onto the couch. I helped her to the bathroom and up the carpeted stairway. We made sloppy love. Tonee asked me for some Vodka.

"No, go to sleep Baby."

She curled on her side as I lay behind her. In the dead of night, I heard her get up and rushed to meet her as she reached the top of the stairs, taking her first step into midair. I caught her by her shirt and held her up before she fell. I walked her down to the bathroom. My heart was racing at the thought of her tumbling down the stairs.

Tonee wanted a drink. I got her some water. I half carried her up the stairs and listened as her breathing slowed to snoozing. In the morning, we snuggled. Tonee showered and left. Sunday was her laundry day, walking down the steepest steps to the basement. I wished she lived with me and didn't have to work so hard for her Mother, but I admired her caring and was glad she had reunited with her Mama.

We talked through the week. Tonee apologized for being such poor company and promised to make it up with a Spaghetti Bolagnese dinner, my favorite. I asked her to please not bring more hard liquor to my house. I was afraid I would get too used to it again and I was afraid she would hurt herself falling. We agreed on Friday night. Tonee said she'd have plenty of energy because she was taking a vacation day.

Tonee came over and started sauteeing her vegetables and taking the fat out of the meat. She looked more rested. I heard her singing to the cats in the kitchen. I went in once and was met with the look and the "I'll bring you anything you want, but stay out of my kitchen."

I could see her working on her Vodka from last week, but I didn't know she'd brought a new bottle. About an hour and a half into prep, I heard a little crash and "I'm okay. I'll bring you dinner now."

A minute later, she stumbled into the living room with a bowl of Bolagnese, setting it down for me as she crashed to the floor. I helped her to the couch where she collapsed to sleep, her shirt fully stained with dinner.

The kitchen was a horror. A full bowl of pasta lay smashed on the floor. The fat cats were happy with red sauce faces. Tonee's drink sweated half empty on the counter.

Dinner was delicious. Kitchen cleanup was intense. I poured a stiff snifter of scotch from last weekend's bottle. Tonee lay asleep, giggling with dreams. I watched TV and drank, Freddie on my feet and Pita in the dominant lap spot. They were my sanity. After a couple of hours, I tried to get Tonee upstairs, but she wouldn't budge. I covered her with an afghan knitted years back by my Mother. I lay down on the recliner, closing my eyes.

Tonee woke while I slept, crashing onto the coffee table, waking me to death. I sat her back on the couch.

"Are you okay Baby?"

"Just hit my head. No problem."

I helped her to the bathroom and up the stairs. I helped her change her shirt for a clean t shirt. I offered some water.

"I want a real drink."

I lay beside her rubbing her head and shoulders till she snored. I could feel energy pulsing in her beautiful head. I rubbed till they subsided. I helped her downstairs to pee in the middle of the night. In the morning, she was anxious to leave.

"I don't want to anger Mama. I didn't tell her I was coming over."

I told Tonee we needed to talk.

"Are you mad at me?"

"No Baby. I could never be angry with you."

Tonee agreed to come back after her Saturday chores. I was happy to be able to see her two nights in a row. I thought about dumping the Vodka and Scotch, but did not do sacrilege. I finished cleaning the kitchen, showered, and left for work.

I wanted to call Tonee at 6pm, but did not. Around 7, the phone rang.

"Hello."

"Hi Bobbie, it's me. I just wanted to make sure you okay." The voice was high pitched, young and soft.

"Who's this?"

"It's me silly, Tonee. Are you ok?" I began to shiver with the beauty and innocence of that voice. I didn't know what to say.

"You sound real different. You said you'd come over tonight. Are you coming?"

"No I didn't. I go to bed soon."

The young voice seemed hurt by my accusation. I held back. She was so sweet and caring. I just wanted to reach out and hug her.

"Listen Tonee, we need to learn to talk clearer to each other. Okay?"

"Okay Bobbie. I go now. BaBye."

"Bye bye Tonee. I love you."

I felt a shock teasing my gut. That little voice, the little girl. Tonee? My heart cried to the voice of that beautiful child. I sucked a little Scotch and had the last of the pasta. I wondered how much wilder my world could become. Was she playing a game with me? Where was her Mother when she called? The phone was right by the spot where Mama roosted. Didn't she hear that voice?

I waited a half hour before I called back. Tonee answered "Hello" in her deep and beautiful voice. I asked her what was going on. She didn't understand. She hadn't called at all today, and, no, she never said she'd come over. I asked her where her Mother was.

"Right here. It's time for Columbo."

I didn't want to ask her more questions with her mother there. I didn't want any confrontation.

"Can you call me later Tonee? I'm very confused. We need to talk Baby."

20

"Okay Robert."

I said goodnight to the last of the Scotch and hugged my pussycats. The sweet darling who called me tonight echoed in my mind. My beautiful, wonderful Tonee was testing the edges of my soul. I went to the kitchen and took the Vodka out of the freezer, chilling my nasty confusion into an easy stupor.

Tonee called me back an hour later. She didn't remember telling me she'd come over tonight. She didn't remember calling me earlier. She didn't say that it didn't happen.

"Tonee, I love you. We need to talk. I need to understand what's happening to you so I can help, so we don't hurt each other unnecessarily."

"Okay Bobbie. We'll set a time to sit down and talk. I love you."

What I hadn't told Tonee was her little girl on the phone absolutely melted my heart. I would do anything to protect her.

I had the conversation with Tonee I'd never imagined having with anyone.

When we sat down to talk over lunch in the middle of the week, Tonee had no memory of the first phone call Saturday. She did not deny it may have occurred.

"That must have been the six year old. She's such a sweet, caring girl. She likes you a whole lot."

The words came from her mouth to my ears. I felt like I was floating in a dream. I had to hug her.

"Wow. What do you mean, your six year old?

21

How many girls are there?"

Tonee looked relieved as she spoke to me about the personalities in her head, most of them very young. She didn't know exactly how many, but more than ten. She told me about the voices echoing in her head throughout her day, inputting their own take on issues large and small. She called them the Committee. All the voices were Tonee, different ages and attitudes, sometimes taking over as needed. Tonee said she sometimes had control over the change, but usually not. She said it would often happen that people told her about a happening or conversation that she had no memory of.

"Well, that's as clear as not." I quipped. I started to question more, but Tonee shut me down.

"I don't want to talk more now Robert. It's giving me an awful headache. Don't be angry."

"I can't be angry with you. I love you Tonee. Just let me know how I can help."

Our next date was an invite from Mama for dinner Saturday night. I brought a red and a white wine, but Tonee and Mama were working on their Vodka with cranberry juice. I kissed Mama on her cheek. Tonee looked pretty, but tired and nervous. Mama had made the sides. She moved with her walker to the kitchen to check on them. Tonee was basting the roast for the final thirty minutes cook time. I couldn't enter the kitchen zone.

Mama tried to engage my conversation. I gave her yes and no answers.

I asked Tonee to show me the house that Mama took over after the death of her third husband, Eddie. Mama was in between husbands after Gil had died of a heart attack. She came from Pennsylvania to the funeral of Eddie's wife, a cousin, and never left, making Eddie husband number three. The tv and dining room were in the new addition. Mama slept on a bed in a side room on the first floor since her legs went bad. The old house had small rooms and crooked floors. The toilet on the first floor was so tiny, I could barely get in. I saw the basement with the almost vertical steps where Tonee had to bring laundry up and down. There was a large freezer in the basement filled with leftovers, clearly marked and dated. Mama did not throw anything out.

We walked up the steep, narrow stairs to the second floor. There were three tiny bedrooms. Tonee showed me the little room with the stuffed closet and her twin bed that was perfectly made.

"I've never slept in the sheets since day one. I just lie on the bed with a blanket."

I couldn't understand how Tonee handled the steep stairs. It must have frightened her. Tonee said she would show me the big new barn after dinner.

We ate dinner with Bonanza blasting. Mama talked through dinner. She had the same husky voice and laugh that Tonee usually had. She had recently given up her cigarettes after seventy years of smoking. Tonee told me her Mother had her light cigarettes in her own mouth in the car when she was six and hand the lit cigarette to her Mother while she was driving so she had continuity. I congratulated Mama on quitting cigarettes. I so wished Tonee would follow.

Dinner was fine. I sipped my wine, but held back because I was driving. Mama had made a special dessert for me which was a chocolate moose and cool whip swirl. She wanted me to take the huge bowl home. The chocolate was great, but I hated the artificial Cool Whip.

"Thank you Mama for the great dinner and the dessert."

Tonee started to clean up. I helped with the plates and offered to wash the dishes.

"Sit down and talk to Mama."

Ziggy climbed onto my lap. Gunsmoke time volume nine. Tonee finally finished. Her shirt was stained. She was sweating. We walked outside into the cool air to see the barn which was separated by thirty yards from the house.

"Sometimes, we see bears and foxes in the yard. One morning, a little bear cub came right to the window where Mama sits."

The barn was newer, built to house Eddie's antique cars. When Eddie was alive, up to nine years ago, some of the trucks from his oil business were kept there. The oil business went to Eddie's brother, Dick, on the cheap. Tonee said her Mother made Eddie put Tonee in his will for a portion of the house with his three children. It was one of the better things I'd heard about Mama.

A replica Model A and an old firetruck were in the barn. An old wooden harpoon hung on the wall. Tonee said the house and barn were skinned clean by his kids of valuables after Eddie died. She said the children were angry at Mama for turning him into an alcoholic.

There was a separated large room with a door. Tonee and I hugged and sat down on the rug of the room.

"Just relax Baby. You did too much."

"Mama will get mad if we don't go back."

Tonee put her head on my lap. I caressed her head till she was almost asleep. Then we made love, before returning to Mama's glare. Mama wanted me to take the dessert home, but I just took a bowl.

Tonee walked me to the car. She handed me a cardboard box full of old pictures for me to put in my car.

"I wanted you to see pictures of me when I was a plump kid."

We held each other and kissed leaning against my car. I could see dark, angry eyes staring from the kitchen. I so much wanted Tonee home with me. I did not want the separation.

I did not know it at the time, but the era of trench warfare had begun. My beautiful, gentle, brittle woman was the battlefield.

We went a week with no visit, not even the weekend. Tonee said Mama was threatening that "it was her or me that she had to make a decision." What a witch.

I stopped by the house around 5:30 in the afternoon early the week after. I was through with work, expecting that I'd meet Tonee coming in from her long day. Tonee's car was not in the driveway. I walked to the back door where Mama met me and let me in.

Mama talked about how proud she was of Tonee's work and how nice it was to have her home again. I was a little nervous and kind of stretched my neck a couple of times. Mama asked if I was okay. I told her my neck was stiff from tension at work. She offered to massage my neck a couple of times. I thought that was nice but weird. I declined. Tonee arrived and was surprised and happy to see me. She smelled heavily of cigarette.

I reminded her of the wine tasting we were invited to on Thursday night. She had agreed to go.

Mama told her my neck was stiff and I'd refused her neck rub. I stayed a little while, was offered dinner, but did not accept. I just needed my Tonee fix.

Tonee walked me to the car and asked me not to stop by unannounced again. She said it creeped her out thinking of her Mother massaging my neck. She told me that years back, she had a boyfriend who had been to the house a couple of times when Tonee wasn't there, but her Mother was.

Tonee was all excited when she came on Thursday. She wore a revealing black knit sweater and was looking remarkably beautiful and young. I invited her upstairs.

"I'd love to, but we'd be late. I have something to show you."

She had a surprise. We went to the trunk of her car where Tonee had an antique bronze angel she had been saving up to buy. It was a couple of feet tall and beautiful and amazingly heavy.

"I want to keep it here." She said "This is home. I call it Poppy."

I brought it to the living room. It was an exact copy of a gift her Father had given her years back and told her never to lose.

The wine tasting was dull. We were both tired by the time we left. I found a spot at the top of the stairs on the landing in front of the great window for her prized Poppy.

We went to bed. I snuggled up to her for a kiss. Tonee seemed tense. She had looked so beautiful all night, I had been lusting for her. Tonee pushed me away, the first time she'd ever refused my advance. In the morning, she woke early and went to work.

We did not see each other that weekend.

Mama was on the Bobbie warpath. We had plans to visit an old friend of mine from High School at their summer home in the Catskills the following weekend. I wondered how Mama was taking the news that Tonee would be gone all weekend.

Tonee came over with a little suitcase and a smile. She said prayers before lighting Shabbos candles. We went out to a nice Chinese restaurant, came home and made love into the night.

Tonee had a portable navigation system that worked well till we were almost at Rick and Lisa's house in the Catskills. It took a couple of phone calls and ignoring the gps which kept bringing us to the wrong street. We finally pulled up to the two hundred year old farmhouse with a huge backyard. Rick came out and greeted us. I hadn't seen him in twenty years. We were all getting older, but Rick was a runner and always lifting weights. We played frisbee in the back yard. I met Lisa, a beautiful Scandinavian blonde who worked at the UN. Rick was an attorney who was "overpaid" for what he did. I knew him when his hair was halfway down his back.

The plan was for Lisa to go to the local stores and shop for dinner ingredients. Rick was a home gourmet cook and gave her details for her shop. We had small salads for lunch. I always remembered him as extreme ADD and unable to properly sleep at night. He hadn't changed.

I asked Rick about the animals next door. We all walked out and took a visit to Jonah's Ark. The huge yard of the old house next door was fenced in. Walking around were Bison and Emu and Elk and Yak and deer. A Giraffe poked its head over the fence looking for food. Rick had brought a few carrots which he gave to Tonee, asking her to be careful of the electrified fence. A Llama nestled in and Tonee fed her a carrot through the fence. The next time she tried it, Tonee sparked on the wire, jumping back, laughing. We walked further down the road before returning so Rick could begin his prep work for dinner.

"Dinner will be served at 6:30. Very informal. Please bring your appetites."

Tonee and I went upstairs to our little room which was beautifully set up like a B&B. right down to the little soaps and shampoo. We had our private bath. We showered and lay down to rest. Tonee seemed at ease in the country, comfortably distant from the pressures of home. I admired the beautiful youth in her face as she slept to dream.

I rested, then walked downstairs to see the old house and talk to Rick as he played cook. Lisa came back, but had to substitute on the type of fish. Rick had a little hissy, then settled in and kissed Lisa and thanked her for the food. I popped the cork on an old merlot I had brought, to let it breathe to be ready for dinner.

Rick got a kick out of the breathing wine. He no longer imbibed, having learned his Irish drinking days proved him an angry drunk. He did hint at the existence of herb beyond the beautiful flavors in the food he was preparing.

I opened another red wine and sipped on that as I watched the master cook.

When I went upstairs to get Tonee, I could hear her crying.

"Fuck Mama."

Apparently she hadn't told her Mother we would be away. Tonee hung up the phone, shaking, ashen. I hugged her and held her. The sun was setting. Rick called the fifteen minute warning. Tonee shook her head and smiled.

"Let's have fun tonight Bobbie."

Dinner was amazing. Tonee ate half her food, a great compliment to the cook. I finished her plate. Rick and Lisa excused themselves to clean up.

The night was full of wine and talk, Rick holding court, melifluous on many subjects. Tonee was exceptionally well read. They talked books. I'd brought a couple of red wines and a couple of white. One of the white wines was well aged and had been highly recommended. It turned out a superb flavor that Lisa and Tonee fully enjoyed.

I was well into my wine when Rick pulled out a joint and lit it. I used to be quite a pot smoker, but hadn't touched it in years. I kept hearing that pot was getting better. Tonee and I took a couple of hits. I could feel my head rising and floating in a very nice way. Rick said something funny as I was swallowing some red wine. I remember choking and spitting wine all over. The next thing I remembered was Rick slapping my back and looking terrified into my eyes.

"Are you Okay?"

"Yeah."

"You gave us quite a scare Robert."

Tonee held me looking frightened. I was light headed. The evening came to a rapid halt.

"Don't ever scare me like that Bobbie. I don't want to lose you. I love you." I scared all the Tonee girls. We made love and fell asleep.

I got up in the middle of the night and didn't want to wake Tonee. I went downstairs where Rick was reading in the kitchen.

"Still an insomniac?"

"You remembered."

Rick and I talked for a while. He was missing his son, Dylan, from his first marriage. He and his ex did not separate well. His son was in High School. His Mother fought Rick for his time.

The morning was a light breakfast and coffee. Rick said they usually headed back to the city by noon, after intaking six pounds of Sunday Times. We had hugs and kisses and said goodbye.

Tonee wasn't feeling well. She didn't know what was wrong. I figured she was shook up anticipating shit from Mama. She didn't want to rest when we returned home. We hugged and she left.

"I had good time Bobby, but I not feel good."

"Good luck with Mama."

The next week was not a good Tonee time. Mama threw her shit fit. Tonee was grounded. She went to the doctor who said she had a urinary tract infection. It was painful and sapped her energy. The real kicker was her finally getting fired from the TV station. Tonee's immediate boss hated her and her expensive salary with commissions.

"Are you okay Baby?"

"No. I can't stand you and Mama pushing me."

Tonee was depressed and hurting and didn't want company. Her Mother was giving Tonee ultimatums that it was either her or me. I felt like I was back in high school. The phone was right at the kitchen table with an 8ft cord, so Tonee had little privacy.

"I love you Bobbie. I don't know what to do."

"We belong together Baby. I'll take care of you."

"I want to be near you, but I don't feel good."

"I can pick you up if you want. You won't have to drive."

This went on for a couple of weeks. Tonee applied for unemployment. I was invited over for

Thanksgiving dinner. Tonee asked if I had any special requests. I told her I love pumpkin pie. It was over two weeks since I saw her last. She was getting over her infection. I missed my woman.

I suppose it's possible I went over for Thanksgiving with an attitude. I kissed Mama on her cheek. I gave Tonee a great hug and kiss. She was nervous, rushing from the kitchen to the tv room getting things perfect. The room was smoky as Tonee kept basting her turkey breast. Tonee and Mama drank vodka and cranberry juice. I opened a Bourdeaux for myself. Ziggy wanted attention and was so soft on my lap. Even Chloe came over for attention. Mama liked football, so we were without Bonanza.

Mama made polite talk. I was just a little ruder and less responsive than normal. I kept looking at Mama and wondering what kind of woman pulls these ultimatums on her very grown daughter. Selfish bitch. Tonee went outside in the cold to smoke. I hated the smoke and the sight of her smoking, but I went with her for our little bit of privacy.

"How do you feel Baby?"

"Not good. I should be in bed. I'm so tired."

Tonee looked worn and old. She was very pale.

"I love you Tonee."

"Me too."

Mama's glare met us as we came in from the cold. She finished her crossword puzzle. Tonee freshened her drink.

"I'm gonna get her set." Tonee gave her a heavy hand on the Vodka.

Dinner was okay, not her best. We had some of the old chocolate moose/cool whip concoction that came up from the freezer. Mama didn't like pumpkin pie so we had none. It pissed me off. The tv was loud and the games were lousy. I felt ornery. I gave the two pussycats the same head shake I always did with my two cats, scrambling their brains just a little. Ziggy was okay, but Chloe went into coughing convulsions. Mama yelled at me.

"You stay away from my cats."

She tried to comfort Chloe, till he finally settled down. Tonee was very upset with me.

"How could you be so stupid?"

I finished my glass of wine and offered Tonee my help cleaning up.

"Leave her alone. She's sick. She's going to bed." Mama politely told me to leave. I kissed Tonee goodbye, put on my coat and left. The coat smelled of Turkey smoke and grease. Tonee gave me a little turkey for my honkers.

"Sorry, I wasn't trying to hurt him."

"That was stupid Bobbie. He's an old cat. You could have killed him."

I was off from work that Sunday. Tonee finally came over. She brought her Vodka and cigarettes. I agreed she could smoke off the back porch. I made bacon and eggs for our dinner. Tonee was distracted and tired. Her skin was silvery pale. She sucked down her Vodka.

Tonee said she was going crazy without a job, even if she had been fluffing her time at work before they fired her. It was the principle of work.

"Mama is driving me crazy. I can't be with her all day, every day. She doesn't want me to see you. I don't know what to do. She's saying it's you or her. I can't stand the pressure."

"I love you Tonee. Your Mother shouldn't say things like that. Stay with me. You can bring Ziggy over. You can visit your Mother and do her chores."

"I love you Robert. My Mother needs me. I came here to be with her and take care of her, to make up for our time apart. I don't know what to do. It's killing me."

"You're not her slave."

"Stop talking Bobbie. I'm tired. Hold me."

Tonee went upstairs to bed early. I went up to cuddle. She didn't want sex. I held her and lay next to her and rubbed her head till she fell asleep.

I went downstairs to TV and Honkers.

I dozed off, kicking awake to Tonee screaming from the bedroom upstairs.

"Robert. Are you there?" She sounded scared.

"I'm here baby?"

"Robert, where are you?" The voice grew louder and deeper. I started to rise.

"You fucking selfish asshole. Where the fuck are you?" I barely recognized the awful voice. She came down the stairs ripping mad.

"It's okay Baby. I'm here. I love you."

"You love yourself you selfish shit. My Mother was right. You only care about your needy cock."

I tried to hug her. I tried to kiss her. I tried to keep her from hitting and spitting and scratching me, but she kept attacking. She was a nightmare come to life.

"I'm done with it. I'm sick of lies, you worthless shit. I'm out of here. Don't stop me."

Tonee walked back to the top of the stairs and picked up her Poppy. She carried him down with one arm on the heavy bronze against her chest and one on the railing to the bottom of the stairway till she put it down to rest. She put on her hat and coat and shoes.

"I'll come back for Poppy. We're through."

Tonee never drove at night. It was icy on the stairs and in the street. I tried to hug her and help her down the front steps. She pushed me away.

"We're done. You and I are none. Nothing. Zero. History. I hate you. Don't ever call me again. Ever."

Can't say she didn't leave with a little Mama drama. This was my first encounter with Bad Tonee on her feet. I was crushed. I couldn't understand what had just happened. My love was gone, hating me. I watched as her car lights left the driveway and passed down the street.

I didn't sleep at all. I drank too much wine. Her Mother kept answering the phone the next day, refusing to let me speak to her daughter. I went to work exhausted and angry and sad. The Finance Manager, who I despised, got in my face over some stupid shit that was none of his business. I told him to go fuck himself. The next day, I was called into the Sales Manager's office and was fired. I told him he owed me my year end bonus and my two weeks vacation pay. He said he would take care of it. I couldn't tell if I felt good or bad as I left the building. I had made the mistake the month before of telling him I wasn't sure if I would stay the next year. I wasn't certain what I would be doing in my near future. Really, all I could think about was my Tonee.

Tonee finally answered my call a couple of days later. She was barely whispering as if talking was a physical effort. She thought it might be best if we didn't see each other. I kind of made a joke about the two of us on unemployment. She reacted very badly to my getting fired.

"I'm not going to support you. Don't ever think you can live off me. You're as bad as my ex." Her voice sounded hurt. She hung up and would not pick up the phone again that day.

I found out that by being fired two weeks before the year ended, I was screwed out of my vacation pay and a years vetting on the 401k. The good news was collecting unemployment was enough to carry me frugally through to my decision towards my future. I could finally sit back and relax. Life could be good if I had my baby back.

Tired of being put off on the phone, I drove to see Tonee at the old farmhouse. Mama scowled from her seat. Tonee wouldn't let me in the house. She came out into the cold. She would not hug or kiss me. She looked matronly and tired and sickly.

"I don't know what's happening Robert. Mama wants to call the cops. You and Mama are killing me. I can't handle this. It's best if we just let it go."

"I love you Tonee. Let me take care of you."

"You can't even take care of yourself. I need to go inside and sleep."

"Do you still love me Tonee?"

"I don't know. I can't think anymore. I hate this shit."

My unemployment kicked in. I got my final checks from work. I had some money saved. I could survive the six months or so available for collecting benefits. The government even helped with health insurance. I was still wanting to leave the area where the economy was down so badly. Israel and Hawaii were both 5700 miles in opposite directions and temperament. I wanted Tonee with me on my journey.

My pussycats were loving my extra time with them. Their attention could not relieve my loneliness and the worry I had that my fragile woman was falling apart without me there to help. I could only imagine the harm her mother was delivering. I wanted her with me, to hold her, to help her, to protect her, to complete us. I went to the library and brought home several books on DID, Disassociative Identity Disorder.

Tonee called a couple of days later and asked if she could come over to talk. I was happy and worried that this visit would be her last.

Tonee came over the next day in the brisk, overcast afternoon. I met her by the car and held her arm up the stairs. She was uneasy on her feet. We sat on the couch. Tonee was not angry, but sad. She was talking as if her speech was prepared, that the sum of things was not positive for us, that the feud with me and her Mother was tearing at her and she could not handle the conflict any more. Her Mother was in her eighties and needing care and attention from her daughter who had been away too long.

"I love you Tonee. I need you. I want you. I want to take care of you. Your Mother will only make you sicker."

"That's not your call."

"Do you still love me Tonee?"

"I don't know anymore. I'm going to leave you. I guess we're through. Please don't call anymore."

Her words ripped into me. I could feel my body lose it's mind, watching this loss from the other side of the room. My love was talking to me for the last time. The smell of her. The smile. The beautiful touch. The intelligence racked in pain. I was helpless watching as she stood and headed for the door. I picked up Poppy, struggling with the weight. I walked behind Tonee to her car. Poppy lay on its side in her trunk. Tonee hesitated by her car, looking at me, shaking.

"I do love you Robert." Her voice was soft, almost silent. "I don't want to lose you. I don't know what to do."

We hugged and shared a gentle kiss. She was shaking and crying.

"I love you Tonee. Let me help you."

"I need to go. I love you Robert. I want you to be with me."

I felt the world trying to set itself right. My hurt twisted to hope. I wanted to laugh and cry.

Tonee waved as she backed down into the street. Our love would find stronger times. Our two unsettled tortured souls might reach a time and place of peace. I needed to help her to help me.

Tonee got weaker and more depressed over the next several days. She spent most of the day and night upstairs in bed. Her Mother said she needed her rest, but she let me in the door when I came over. I climbed the steep stairs to her room. She lay on top of her sheets, crying. She looked old and tired in the sparse light. I rubbed her head which throbbed in different places.

The next time I came over, Tonee was sitting at the table downstairs. Her Mother was watching The Rifleman, ignoring me. I held Tonee's hands and spoke to her and looked into her deep blue eyes.

"Things will be better my love."

Mama coughed.

"I love you Tonee. You'll feel better soon." I

rubbed her head and shoulders till Mama kicked me out.

"She needs her rest."

Tonee's depression went on for three more weeks. My phone rang one afternoon.

"Bobbie, can I come over?" The voice was very young.

"Do you want me to come and get you?"

"Yes please."

Tonee was waiting with a little suitcase and a smile. She looked young and tired, but less worn than before. I kissed her and walked her to my car.

"I want to be with you Bobbie. Don't ever leave me."

She lay down on my couch with a pussycat and a glass of chardonnay.

"Are you hungry Baby?"

"Just hold me Bobbie."

I sat with her head in my lap. I did not know if her little tears were happy or sad.

"I love you beautiful girl. We need to be together."

For the first time in a long while, I could feel my life beginning to breathe again.

Tonee slept till dusk. I helped her upstairs and held her as she cried herself back to sleep.

"Are you okay Baby?'

"I'm ok Bobbie."

She slept deep into the night, sometimes kicking and moaning and mumbling, sometimes giggling. In the deepest night, she was silent and calm.

In the morning, I helped her downstairs to the shower. Tonee took her time. She was singing. I heard the blow dryer. The waft of perfume scented through the door. She sang an old children's song emerging fresh and alive, her husky voice demanding a kiss. We went out in the sunny, cold morning for breakfast and coffee. My love was beginning to breathe again the air that angels breathe.

"I need you Bobbie. Thank you for your patience. I didn't mean to hurt you."

Her appetite was good.

"Move in and live with me my love."

"Bobbie, this place is filthy. Nice girls don't live like that."

"Easy to fix. Will you live in my cleaned apartment?"

"Yes."

We loved slowly in the afternoon. I was alive again and my woman was getting healthy. I made a few calls. A nice old lady came in the morning and cleaned and cleaned and came back and cleaned all the next day till the apartment was fit for Tonee. We went back to Mama's and gathered Tonee's belongings for the great transition to be complete. Tonee kissed her Mother, telling her she'd be back to help with the Saturday chores. Mama did not look happy.

Tonee was outside in her car. I was hauling the last bundle of her belongings down the steep steps. Mama put her cane out to stop me. She wore an odd look and a sad voice.

"Congratulations. You won."

I felt bad for the selfish old bitch.

Tonee grew stronger quickly, busy making our apartment prettier. She cooked dinner every night. The comfort of her was healing me.

She went to help Mama Saturday morning, returning in the late afternoon as pale as a ghost,

39

shaking, crying. I held her and hugged her. Why would her Mother treat her so? I could not understand. My little girls and my big girls shook with the hurt. Tonee put her head on my lap and cried. My anger for her Mother festered. I could not understand how such a gentle soul came from that selfish witch.

The early days living with Tonee were sensational. Her love and soul and wit and strength were a pleasure to experience, a constant ride of surprise. She would quote her precious Ellen "It takes a village to care for Tonee?" Tonee was not a low maintenance personality.

My sixty hour work weeks were gone for the first time in five years. My amazing crazy lady and my two honkers were great hangin buddies. There was love and loving, the joy of discovery, the great comfort building within us as we survived two, three weeks, a month together without major damage. We fought or argued over hard liquor and her smoking, and, to some degree, over work. Tonee would spend hours each day on the computer building her resume, sending out applications, despite having her unemployment compensation. The money was half what each of us had been earning, but it was survivable and liveable. I viewed it as a great vacation and a transition as I explored the possibility of moving to Hawaii or Israel. Tonee was afraid I would become lazy and live off her like her last short term husband, Mr. Arkansas. I told Tonee I worked my ass off my whole life and I deserved some rest and time with my beautiful Dove.

Tonee and I had used the M word from early on. It just seemed so strong and crazy wild and smart. Tonee was barely a year back to New England to be with her family and I was talking of pulling her away to be closer to mine. My Father had died last year and my Mother was hoping to die as she was lost in her own body and mind with advanced Parkinsons. I had used my two weeks vacation time and saved money each of the last five years to visit Israel and reacquaint myself with my brothers and their massive families, but specifically to spend as much time as possible with my parents while I still had them.

I called Israel a few times and had Tonee talk to my brothers to get more comfortable. I wanted her to come to visit Israel and see if she would like it and consider a move there. She spoke on the phone with her deep throated, outgoing voice and spoke to the guys longer than I did. She would not commit to a trip in a month or so. I told her I would pay and we could do it on the cheap, living with family. She didn't like that, so I checked on rates for rooms. She seemed intimidated by the ultra orthodox and was afraid she'd be looked down on as a convert and an unwed lover.

My plan was to visit Israel with Tonee and a month or so later, fly out to Hawaii and have her meet my brother, Ken and his wonderful Chinese wife, Lynette. I hadn't seen them in over ten years. Tonee was more amenable to the idea of a tropical visit. But she really wanted to stay in Massachusetts where she had her family and the change of seasons she'd missed for so many years in L.A.

The vodka war was up and down for a few weeks. She'd bring a bottle home and get hammered and sloppy, losing her balance and falling. She fell on the carpeted steps and the bedroom floor a few times, but mostly downstairs on the slick hardwood floors or outside in the back yard where she would get her smokes in. I tried not to ultimatum her, but I was terrified of my own intake and did not want the fall down drunk she'd become with the hard liquor. I remember one day, when she had been drinking pretty hard, she fell asleep, slouched in a chair, with the smile and contented innocent look of a six year old drunk. Tonee finally began to relent and I did my best to keep enough white wine in the house to float a goat.

Tonee's smoking was a tougher story because there was no substitute. She'd been smoking regularly since she was a teen and she loved it. She said she started at six with her Mother driving in their car and Tonee lighting fresh cigarettes in her mouth and passing them on to her Mother. Bad Mommy. Tonee promised to cut down, that the times in the past she tried to stop, never worked. Her Mother had finally stopped smoking this past year after seven decades of the habit. She had the fear of cancer. I wanted Tonee healthy and couldn't stand seeing her smoke. I was surprised she could brush her teeth as well as she did to keep the taste from our kisses.

Tonee would see her Mother two or three times a week to do her chores and stay in touch, but she would always return to me and the Honkers. I was beginning to understand Tonee's sleeping better, her nightmares and amazing dreams, living in the past. She would meet her Father and old friends and relatives and walk into long adventures that she'd describe in the morning. In the depth of the night she would often go into her rem sleep and go further into herself, not to be disturbed. She would describe it as having long ties from her head out into space where little parts of her could rest. She would reel them in, one at a time, as she slowly woke.

I would look at her face while she was asleep and see the different Tonees, some so young and relaxed, some older and afraid. I was always amazed at the great flexibility in her facial features. I loved all the girls, even the Bad Tonees who would rise out of nowhere and inflict their righteous anger and protection. I was getting used to changing the sheets often as she would soil in the night. I picked up a second bed liner so there would be no protection interruptions from the wash cycle.

New Year's eve was kind of a milestone of survival and the hope that our next full year together would bear great fulfillment to our souls. We had nice champagne and cognac. I felt so lucky to be with such a strong woman.

Sometime early that week, we were lying in bed, Tonee looking nervous.
"Are you okay?" I asked her.
"Can I ask you a question? I've been wanting to for a long time now."
"Okay."
"Promise you won't be mad?" She was young and scared.
"I love you."
"Ok. Is it Okay if I call you Daddy sometimes?"
"Of course sweetheart. I love you."
"Thank you Daddy. I'm so happy. It makes me feel real good."
I didn't know what to think of her request. She adored her Father. Most of what I had read about DID personalities involved abuse and or sexual abuse as a child. Tonee had no memory of any sexual abuse. She was alive with the stories of a young girl whose parents fought over her vacation time, of a mother who called her daughter ugly and fat and stupid, of a dumb step mother who did not give her love. She had great stories of her Father and his ingenuity and the

bon vivant step dad who treated her like a loving daughter.

Sometimes, I would ask her about the girls and the committee, but mostly she wasn't comfortable with the talk. Sometimes, I would ask how old she was now and sometimes she would answer. Occasionally, I'd hear the tiny sweet voice of the three year old who everybody protected. Most of the voices were six or ten or sixteen years old. The sixteen year olds were decision makers, smart and driven. I'd hear elegant vocabulary and language style from one. I couldn't distinguish how many bad Tonees there were, but they were the protection squad, scared and angry. Most of the Tonees were young and wonderful.

Tonee remembered stories from her youth in such detail like they just happened with the happiness or anger or sadness still fresh. She would pull old songs or phrasing from nowhere. Her adult years had decades of lost memory. She lived with the love and hurt of her youth. My Baby had a hard, hard start. One day, we looked through her box of old photos. Her Father's Fez from the Shriners lay on top in a plastic bag. Tonee opened it to touch as if it were a shrine. The smell of Aqua Velva still clung to the fabric through the years.

Tonee showed me pictures of her Mother, saying how extraordinarily beautiful she was. One picture showed Mama from the back holding a tiny Tonee like a piece of wood looking at herself in the mirror.

"See how beautiful I am. See how ugly you are." Tonee spoke the words like she heard them yesterday, not as a tiny, plump three year old child.

Tonee loved the picture of her Father in his semi pro football uniform. He was the place kicker.

They called him The Toe.

Tonee started to cry as she showed me picture after picture of little Tonee with her dead eyes, a young child torn between her parents, with the joy of innocence ripped from her soul. All I could do was hold her and kiss her and tell her how much I loved her.

"Thank you Daddee."

Tonee showed me pictures of her early adolescence while she was still plump, but very athletic. There were pictures of her Daddy and Elinor, the step mom. There were a couple of pictures of Tonee with Sandy, her older step sister who she liked.

"They kept forcing me on diets. Why couldn't they just let me grow into my body?"

In early high school, her weight trimmed into her height and her beauty developed into a stunning woman. She was so beautiful.

There were almost no pictures of high school. She went off to College and Grad School, working double jobs to put herself through. The pictures and memories disappeared in her adult years. Tonee married a Jewish boy in her twenties. They did not last long. She'd married again ten years ago in California, a user from Arkansas. She didn't know why she married him. It lasted a year.

From the box of memories emerged a single picture of a huge, sickly black woman.

"This is my beautiful Ellen. I loved her so. We were sisters. You can see the ALS."

The picture was shocking. Tonee didn't speak of her decision when she had to stop caring for Ellen in her own apartment and send her off to a care home. I couldn't imagine the 5'5" 120 lb Tonee being able to lift her Ellen.

January was love month. Tonee refused any talk of her visiting Israel. I needed to see my Mother one last time, as hard as it was in her awful condition. I drove to JFK airport with Tonee by my side. She would drive home alone and pick me up at Bradley in Hartford when I returned in two weeks. I usually flew El Al, but I went with Iberia Airlines to save some money, a big mistake.

Tonee would stay at our house and take care of the Honkers. I was worried about her being in that house in that neighborhood alone. It used to be a beautiful section, but not any longer. I knew she would be spending much of her time at her Mother's. I felt strong for our love, but I feared the black hand of Mama could only do damage.

Tonee was quiet as I drove ever faster as we neared NYC. I could hear her crying. She looked young. We would email daily. We kissed goodbye. I hated leaving her.

The flight was long and horrible, bad plane, bad service, filthy bathrooms that marginally worked. Two of Gedalia's kids met me at Ben Gurion airport. The dry heat of the Israeli winter felt wonderful.

I had been to Israel three times in my life before starting my string of six January visits. The people were nice and very energetic. The country was calmer since the border walls were constructed. My Mother was a Zionist, traveling to Israel for the first time back in 1956 when the country was in its infancy. She held my little brother in her belly. She returned several more times in the years to follow, and eventually influenced Gedalia and then Jeffrey to move and settle. Eventually, when my Father retired, they moved to Israel where they pleasured in the beautiful company of so many grandchildren. My parents had an awful relationship, but they mostly stayed together for almost sixty years.

As we approached the heights of Jerusalem, I got my usual God rush. Something about that old city and its atmosphere always moved my non religious heart. Gedalia lived in the Jewish Quarter in the Old City, three blocks from the Wailing Wall. It was a cool place to be.

As usual, it was great seeing my Brothers and the kids and the grandkids. Each of my brothers had nine children who were reproducing at a clip. Gedalia had volunteered to fly helicopters in Viet Nam when he was barely twenty years old. That year in his life produced great memories of heroism and sacrifice, leaving him disenchanted and sick for the rest of his life. He was ultra orthodox in his own Becker way. He had a good marriage, but was still troubled by health and emotional demons.

My Brother Jeffrey came over for Shabbos. We all went to the Wall for prayers. The plan was that I would borrow my parents' old car and drive to Jeffrey's for a couple of days to watch the Superbowl and then visit our Mother who lived near Hebron, a place I would not travel to on my own.

Jeffrey and I had a good time. I took some of his kids with us for a day sightseeing. He was in the long process of divorce from an awful marriage. Somehow, his kids seemed to have survived. We started watching the game at 3am Israeli time. I was exhausted and barely over my jet lag. I brought Jeffrey a bottle of Laphroig, my favorite Scotch, which he would usually nurse over the year. He had some awful imitation bourbon and Scotch and some Israeli beer. What a nasty combination. I barely slept in his unkempt, dirty apartment that he shared with another divorced guy. When I went to wake Jeffrey at noon, he told me I was crazy. He was too hung over to go see our mother. I was angry and left, heading for Jerusalem, getting badly lost and unnerved, before finally finding the gates of the Old City.

Jeffrey's oldest son, Benny, knew I wanted to visit Hebron. He came over and offered to drive me in the parents' car. All the kids were religious. Benny had finished a stint in the army, but was out now.

I braced myself for the sight of my Mother, but it was never enough. I always pictured her so young, vibrant and beautiful. She had been the source of self and strength for me. Of the six Brothers, I always felt she had a special feel for me which I so needed. She gave us love of nature and animals. She gave me the strength to perform above expectations.

She had been sick and degenerating for eight years. I could only brace myself for the shock of seeing her, weak and emaciated, unable to walk, a look of disorientation and pain in her eyes. I kissed her and held her hand.

"I'm Robert."

She was in her final days. I could not tell if she recognized me. In the last year or two, she came alive for brief moments of clarity and recognition. She had described the torture of her mind and soul lost between worlds. She wanted peace. I stayed with her for two days. One time as I was sitting by her side she spoke clearly for a moment.

"You look much happier than last year."

I could see half a smile in her face. I told her I would marry this beautiful Jewish girl I had met. I don't know if she understood.

"I love you Mommy. Please find your peace."

I tried not to cry in her room. It was time to go. I wanted to return again on this trip, but I knew this might be the last kiss I ever gave her. I cried all the way back to Jerusalem as Benny drove.

Gedalia and I took a trip into the west bank and through Galilee to the mountain top ancient town of Svat, where he had a small apartment to be at peace. This was a famous ancient town, home to the ascetic movement in Israel centuries back where great mystic Rabbis lived amazing lives of dedicated self sacrifice and prayer, reaching as close to God as could be imagined. The cemetery at the base of the mountain was filled with a history of great men. He said this was the only place he could rest. It was nice being with him and enjoying the serenity of this crazy, religious wonderland.

He was excited for me that I had found a good Jewish girl. I told him we were planning a move to Hawaii. I asked if I could have the balance of my inheritance. He agreed. It was not a substantial amount, but it would make things work.

On the ride home, we stopped off at the ancient port of Cesaria, where I'd always enjoyed walking in the Roman Ruins, picking up small pieces of ancient pottery and sculpture from the ground.

My time in Israel was fading. I walked from Gedalia's Jerusalem home out of the Damascus gate and up to King David street where I shopped each year for a few ancient treasures to bring home. Mr Takir, a small elderly man with a quiet voice had been there for decades and had an impeccable reputation. He remembered me and we spent hours in his two story shop. He brought me outside to his storage warehouse. I always asked him to show me his oldest pieces, some dating 5-6000 years old.

I told him I needed to bring my wife a gift of Jewelry. He opened drawer after drawer of rings and necklaces and bracelets, some newer, some ancient. I began to select some pottery and jewelry. I took a picture of a stunning deco bracelet, gold with white sapphire stones which I emailed to Tonee to see if she liked it.

"It's amazing Robert. But we can't afford." was her response.

I came back two more days to fine tune my collection and budget. We agreed on prices. I would take the jewelry by hand. He would mail the pottery USPS. I shook in excitement as I left his place holding some precious gifts for my love. I hoped they would please her. I missed her so much.

On my last day, Gedalia and I took a tour to the ruins below the old city. We saw the old quarry where the huge rocks for the wall had been cut. We walked beneath the old Wall where there was another sixty feet of wall depth in some places. We passed as close as one could get without desecrating the sanctity to where the old temple was believed to have been. I could only imagine the enormity of slaughter that occurred century after century, as one civilization wiped out the other, leveled it and built their own world in this epicenter of Godhood.

It was difficult saying goodbye to my family in Israel. I did not know when, if ever, I would see them again.

The Iberia flight home was a total nightmare. The passengers were rude. The employees were bad. The toilets didn't work before we left. There was a two hour flight delay for engine maintenance. When we landed in Madrid, the Jewish passengers were kept isolated in a secure room. There was detailed reboarding and double checking to make sure all the baggage was proper and identified by passenger. A bomb sniffing dog was the last check. Armed security was everywhere.

We finally landed in New York. I took a shuttle flight to Hartford where I was met in the cold by my beautiful, tearful Tonee. It felt like we were apart forever. The distance melted in a kiss.

I was exhausted and dirty. The Honkers were wild to see me. I showered while Tonee started my special Bobbie Home dinner. We sipped wine and ate her beautiful roasted chicken with potato and brussels sprouts. I dropped a couple of bites for the pussycats.

We made love in the moonlight. I was so tired, but excited. Tonee was like a little girl, so happy I was home.

"Do you want to wait till tomorrow for your gift Tonee?"

"What did you bring me Daddee?" She jumped up and down. Her eyes lit up in the dim light. She followed me downstairs where we sat on the couch and I gave her a little box.

"It's so pretty. Thank you Bobbie." She put the gold butterfly ring with a tiny emerald on her finger.

"I was going to wait till tomorrow for your next gift."

"I don't think so Bobbie."

Reaching into my other pocket, I found a larger box."

"They're so beautiful. " The bracelet was old, white and yellow intertwined gold with natural pearls. They were a perfect fit for her tiny wrists. "I've never seen anything like this."

"They're very old. I can send them back if you don't like."

Tonee didn't like my joke.

"Are you happy Baby?"

Tonee was beaming, but had the what are you hiding look.

"Is that it Bobbie?"

"Yes Baby." My plan was to give her a gift a day. It was difficult holding back. I told her the gold and sapphire bracelet was too expensive.

We drank some more and watched Food Channel before going to bed, to sleep in each other's arms deep into the following morning.

Tonee's bacon and eggs with coffee were a great return from the Israeli Kosher diet. Tonee wore her ring and bracelet.

"What time did you want to open your last gift?"

Her head snapped to serious mode.

"Right now silly."

"Would you like to see your ring or your necklace first?"

Her face was beaming and she jumped up and down, looking to see which pockets were holding gifts for her.

"You have to find them yourself."

Tonee reached into my left pocket and pulled out a ring box.

"My God Bobbie, a diamond. It's so beautiful. I was praying you'd bring me an engagement ring. I love you so much. I can't wait to show Mama."

Tonee was crying. The gold Edwardian ring with three miner's cut diamonds with ruby chips on each corner was sized too big for her fingers. She held it sparkling in the sunlight. After a while, she remembered the necklace question and went digging in my other pocket. The gold chain was lined in 2000 year old ruby beads and gold clusters. It was gorgeous on her neck.

"Thank you Daddee. Is that it?"

I was going to wait till tomorrow, but I was so anxious to see her wear her new jewels. I went to my suitcase and gave her the old ruby bracelet to match the necklace. The clasp was old gold and intricate in design and style. I didn't know how to open it. Tonee figured it out.

"Wowzers. You're amazing. How could you afford it? You shouldn't have." I could see her happy eyes thinking. "How much was the sapphire bracelet? Maybe I could send the money and he could mail it to us."

I went to the kitchen and came back with two glasses of wine.

"It would be too much. I shouldn't have shown you. Are you disappointed Baby. I'm sorry."

"I love you Robert. This is the nicest day I've ever had. Nobody ever treated me like this. Let me see what I can wear with my ruby collection and engagement ring."

Tonee went upstairs and was playing with clothes and her new jewelry when I placed the last little box in her hand.

"I knew it." She said, kissing me as she opened the box with the gold and white sapphire bracelet. "It's amazingly beautiful." Again, her tiny wrists were just perfect for the size.

"Are you happy my love? That's really it Baby. No more."

"You're incredible. I can't believe it. They're all stunning. Who helped you pick these out Bobbie?"

"All me Tonee. I just tried to picture what might be as beautiful as you."

The next few weeks were like a good honeymoon. Tonee brought her booty to show Mama.

"Don't you feel cheated not getting a new ring?" Was her first comment.

Tonee had her rings sized and cleaned and the clasps reinforced on the necklace and bracelets. She agreed to visit Oahu where we could stay with Kenneth and Lynette for a few weeks to see if we might want to move there. I made the plane reservations. Tonee continued to send out job resumes online. My landlord agreed to watch over my cats.

Israel was not a consideration for our move. Tonee had grown up in Pennsylvania and went to College in Philly. I was not interested in Pennsylvania. I was gung ho on Hawaii even though I knew the cost of living would be higher. I figured we could easily survive on two decent incomes.

Tonee made the apartment pretty with knick knacks here and there. My Israeli pottery arrived. The new pieces fit well with my collection. Around the walls were old pictures and art from the home I grew up in.

Tonee wanted an alone room and a rocking chair to soothe her. I asked around and made some calls, finding an antique store. I bought an old rocker with lion head arms and a wicker rocker. I cleared a large space from the front sunroom and gave Tonee a desk to use.

Tonee loved the rockers and used them for one day in the side room. I moved the lion chair into the livingroom to see if she'd use it there. Occasionally, she would use the side room and close the door. I bought her some pastels and paper in case she wanted to draw.

Tonee had good days and a few bad days where she seemed anxious about everything. She had been having her regular doctor prescribe anxiety pills for her. I kept asking her to find a good therapist who could properly prescribe for her. She talked to a couple of people. I asked her to see if anyone local had experience with DID. There was a psychologist in the next town. Tonee met her for the first time before our flight. She liked her a lot.

The plan was to drive to the airport and leave the car in long term parking for the three weeks we were away. Tonee was anxious but positive about the trip. I think she was looking forward to being out of Mama's sight for a while. I don't think she'd told Mama about our trip till the day before we left. I felt a little guilty that she would be alone, but I felt in my gut that she was bad and always had been for Tonee.

Ken and Lynette met us at the airport with leis. We barely recognized each other after more than a decade. I always liked Lynette. Tonee was nervous and tired. We stopped for Thai food on the way to their home on the North Shore. The food was great after a day of nothing but the noise of a jet engine. Tonee barely ate. She held my hand tightly in the car.

Ken was breeding dogs. Everywhere were dogs. The house smelt and I got my first flea bite almost immediately. The main room was the tv room. There were separation sheds for the dogs in heat and the puppies. It was fun seeing the little buggers barely out of the womb. Tonee lit up with the young life.

To my surprise, my oldest Brother, Tommy, was sleeping in the basement. He had snuck out of the care home he was at in Kaneohe. Ken said he'd bring Tommy back the next day. Tommy needed his meds. I hadn't seen him in fifteen years. He was a shock, toothless and head shaved cleaned. He called himself Tony Flowers, my hippie brother who came to the islands forty years ago, living as a paranoid schizophrenic who's adult life was in and out of institutions. He was one of my favorite Brothers, kind and caring. As a kid, his nickname for me was Little Wingbat. He begged a cigarette from Tonee and ran outside to smoke it into the filter. He liked that Tonee and he shared a name. He sat with us in the tv room drinking wine and bumming butts. His finger tips were burnt and stained of cigarette. My brother, Tommy, was an original. Ken said he was much more settled than in his youth when he was a crazy fucker. We talked and laughed. Tonee took a special bond with the Flower. It was a nice surprise seeing him.

By the time we woke early the next afternoon Tony Flowers had returned to his home. I hoped we'd be able to see him again soon.

We stayed in their daughter's room on the main floor. It was comfortable with a little lanai. The floor was elevated. We were at tree top height. Birds chirped in the trees.

Tonee and I slept like rocks the first night. We made love. Tonee had a worried look. I think she was not comfortable out of her own space. We had three weeks to go. My brother, Ken, could be aggressive with his mouth. I hoped we would all get along.

The weather had been unusually wet for the islands. Little did I know that our trip to this paradise would be in the middle of an historic wet pattern. We did get to the beach on the third day. It was the North Shore and Ken had been a surfer, so he didn't know where to go for regular bathing. We went to Pipeline, and then Sunset beach where the rip currents were intense. I went in the water, but Tonee couldn't handle it. She was very uncomfortable on the sloping sand to the water. She had a panic attack. We put off the beach for another day.

Ken and Lynette were good hosts driving us around to see parts of the island, but it was raining almost all the time. We especially liked the shrimp trucks in Kahuku. It was the only time Tonee really dug in to eat.

The highlight of the time was Tonee with the little puppies. She spent hours each day socializing the little buggers. She didn't seem to mind too much getting peed on. I think the little girls in her were in their puppy glory. When Roxie, a young schnauzer, would get in the house, her whole face would light up from the energy.

My Brother used to be a huge asshole, smoking pot all day and arguing just to exercise. Remarkably, he had mellowed immensely and given up on pot. Tonee and I drank our wine. Ken and Lynette mostly were completely sober. As nice as Ken was, he would still get in some digs to get a response from Tonee. She told me she was getting tired of it. We were there about nine days, with just two half days of sun. I tried to get Tonee out of the house to drive around and get a feel for different parts of the island, but mostly she didn't want to go out in the rain. Remarkably, she was making phone calls and submitting resumes locally. She asked me to take her into town one day for an interview for Yellow Page advertising. We left early so we'd have time to get lost. Tonee looked so serious and prepared in her cream white business suit. We reached Honolulu, found the street, and found some parking. I walked her to the outside of the building. She asked me to wait downstairs. She went up the elevator and came back down an hour and a half later with a great Tonee smile.

"I got the job. The next campaign starts in early summer."

What a woman. We celebrated the event with a good bottle of wine and some Kahuku shrimp. Ken and Lynette were very surprised. My beautiful baby came, saw and conquered.

Ken raised little dogs which were popular on the island, Papylon, miniature Schnauzer, miniature poodle and silky Terrier. There was one three month old female Schnauzer that was an outside dog that Tonee fell in love with. That was Roxie. She would be breeding in about six months. Tonee hugged and held Roxie each day she'd sneak in.

"Bobbie, can I have her?"

It didn't make sense to get Roxie and pay to bring her home just to bring her back. There were also quarantine issues. I promised Tonee a puppy if we came back to Oahu to live.

Ken had been telling us about an evening buffet in town that was to die for. He made reservations for all of us. Tonee had seemed a little ancy the last day or two. She complained to me about Ken's mouth. I tried to tell him to be very easy with her. We were ten days into our visit and we'd barely seen much of the island. There were road closures and flooding all over. The four of us and all the puppies and dogs and dog shit and fleas were stuck in the house breeding a need for private space.

It was raining slightly the night of the buffet. Tonee and I cuddled in the back seat. She looked beautiful in her white slacks and pink shirt. She wore a pink denim jacket. She had on her ruby necklace and bracelet and the sapphire bracelet on the other wrist. As always, she displayed her diamond ring with pleasure. She was in a good mood.

The buffet was nice. I tuned in on the lamb chops which were ordered from the table. Tonee poked away at some good sized shrimp. Ken and Lynette are very slow eaters. I was usually done first. The waiters brought out a fresh tray of crab legs to the buffet table. Ken asked for a couple of claw crackers. He joked about bringing the metal crackers home and Tonee got into the play, taking a cloth napkin and wrapping one to take with her. Ken and Lynette left for more food. Tonee had her teenage beautiful face and she was giggling. I asked her not to take the cracker. She was surprised, her eyes rapid blinking, and then she turned away angry and quiet. She pushed my hand as I tried to hold her.

"Don't get angry Tonee. I love you."

Tonee was silent all the way home. She wouldn't let me touch her in the back seat. I could see her dark eyes in the dim light. She wouldn't let me help her up the unsteady walk to the house. Lynette helped her. This was the first angry Tonee I'd seen in a while. In the house, she stormed to the bedroom, showered and went to sleep. I stayed up to watch a movie with Ken. I sipped some wine, hoping a happy Tonee would greet me in bed.

Tonee wouldn't let me near her. She went into her prolonged "selfish Robert" rant and told me she was going home in the morning "to live with Mama." All I could ever do was to back off and hope a good Tonee would wake in the morning.

At dawn, Tonee packed her clothes. She told me to drive her to the airport, that "We were through, done, finished." My heart dropped. I tried to talk to her, but she threatened to hit me and scream if I got near her.

Lynette was up before Ken. I asked her if I could borrow a car to take Tonee to the airport. Lynette was surprised and asked if she could help. I told her Tonee got moody sometimes.

I found the airport without getting lost. Tonee was silent and wouldn't respond. She looked tired and sad and confused and old. I asked if she had her flight set. She told me not to worry about her "ever again."

"I guess this is goodbye Robert."

Tonee gave me a quick stare and left through the glass doors. I kept hoping she would turn around. I thought this might be the last time I ever saw her. My heart and head and brain were in a major shitter. I cried as I drove back to Haleiwa in the rain. I picked up plenty of wine and returned to the house and the barking dogs, depressed and confused.

Ken and Lynette were very surprised. I told them she was worried about her Mother and that maybe Ken had irritated her a little too much. I finished a bottle of wine with a peanut butter sandwich and went back to bed, hoping Tonee would call from the airport for help.

I couldn't sleep. Tonee didn't call. I looked around at the mess she had left on her side of the room. There were still some of her clothes filled with her scent. I lifted her hat on the counter and found her little jewelry box. It still held most of the Israeli gifts. I found her engagement ring under her pillow on the bed. I should have been used to Tonee trauma, but I loved her so much, I couldn't handle the thought of losing her.

Ken and Lynette took me around the ocean drive to the Windward side of the island. The day was nasty with heavy wind and rain. When we reached Kaneohe, we stopped in to see Tommy. We took him out to McDonalds, set him up with a pack of smokes and left him off at the home. Ken said Kaneohe and Kailua nearby would be good places to consider. They were an easier commute to Honolulu than most of the island and the population might be friendlier than the Leeward side or the North Shore. Everything looked bleak and weather worn. I wondered how much harsher the windward side might be. The Koolau mountains were spectacular, alive with waterfalls. I appreciated the day out of the house where Tonee's perfume still filled the sheets.

Tonee had been gone three days. I still had a week to go. I didn't know what to do. I checked my email daily. To my delight, an email came from my love. She was sorry and apologetic, asking me not to be angry and to forgive her. I emailed back that I could never be angry with her. We stayed in contact till I flew back to the cold Northeast. I thanked my host and hostess. They wished me luck and hoped we would move out to their Island.

Once again, I spent a long day flying and sitting in airports. My car was waiting for me in the airport parking. It started up on that frozen evening after a little groaning. I had to be careful not to speed too much as I raced home to my woman and pussycats. Tonee was beautiful and warm. I needed her so much. The pussycats were all over me. I was home. Tonee seemed a little nervous. She said her mother was pushing her again to give me up, back to her threatening.

"It's him or me."

Tonee and I lay in bed talking and loving. She was a little sheepish when I gave her back her jewelry.

"I was afraid I had lost them. I didn't want to tell you."

The world was resetting itself. I could not imagine my life without her again, every funky, erratic part of her. Tonee had warned me early on she would be the craziest woman in my life. Yippeeyayee! I was in for a wild Tonee ride. Her prophecy was spot on.

I can't say it took a few days to get back to normal with Tonee. I'm not sure there is such a state. We talked a lot about the near future and about getting married. I told Tonee that I would like Rabbi Edelman to marry us. He had always been nice to me and often invited me for Shabbat Services and dinner at his home. He and his wife had been a great comfort to me during my hardest days.

I wanted to go ahead with the Hawaii move. Tonee was not crazy about the idea, but said she would go if I really wanted it. I had never lived outside the Springfield area. The local economy was not good and long term area prospects were not strong. I was still very embarrassed by my business failure and legal issues. I needed a change. I thought we could live better and have a good life in the tropics. I also thought her mother would be a long term negative factor to Tonee. All the books I had read on DID related to negative childhoods and usually some level of sexual abuse. Tonee had no memory of sexual abuse from her childhood, but she was filled with negative memories of her parents fighting over her and the negative constant input from her Mother and step mother. Mama was a scary person to me. She was fighting for her own selfish needs and seemed to have little interest in Tonee's wants or needs.

After visiting with my brother Tommy, aka Tony Flowers, a couple times in Hawaii, I began having a tougher time calling Tonee by her name. I began using Baby and My love and other phrases more often. I didn't know if Tonee had noticed.

I brought Fred and Pita to the vet to have their blood drawn and checked for Rabies. This was a four month process before we could send them to Hawaii without quarantine. The tests were expensive. I suggested to Tonee that she have Ziggy done, but she hesitated even when I offered to pay. She didn't know how old Ziggy was, at least ten years, and how much longer he would live. She also did not want to take Ziggy from her mother who was very fond of the cat. I suggested we try to bring Ziggy over and see how she got along with my cats. We tried that a couple of times. Ziggy was very cool and outgoing, but Fred and Pita wanted nothing to do with a new cat in their house.

Tonee and I got friendly with Tommy and Lisa from the antique store. We kept buying things, thinking it would be cheaper here than in Hawaii. Tonee kept telling me to stop, but I loved the look on her face when she had something new that she liked.

Tonee kept sending out resumes and going for interviews. If we moved to Hawaii, it would be the end of June or early July after the blood work was done for the cats. Tonee was insisting we have a place to stay and I have a job before she would agree to move. She was checking for apartments in Oahu on the internet. I told her we could stay with Ken and Lynette for a little while, that it would be easy to find an apartment once we were there. I also thought my getting a job as a car salesman would be quick and easy. Tonee was insistent. I made reservations for a two week stay for myself starting the end of May. I called and let Ken and Lynette know. They said I would have to get a rental car. The cost of this extra trip was worrying me with our transition budget to Hawaii. This would be my third long trip in five months. I was getting to hate these long sleepless flights. I could feel the miles stiffening the spine on my back.

Tonee heard from an old friend of her's and

Ellen's. It was Vicki calling from California to tell
Tonee that Ellen had left a piece of artwork for her.
Vicki didn't have the money to send it.
Tonee sent out some money and then got another call
a couple of weeks later. Vicki wanted $125
more for her time and the shipping costs. Tonee said
Vicki was one of her and Ellen's lost girls in California,
barely surviving off their street savvy. Apparently,
Vicki was selling stock over the phone for oil wells.
Tonee declined the stocks, but sent the extra money,
insisting Vicki follow through this time. A package
arrived cod a couple of weeks later containing a neat,
funky, art nouveau sculpture made by a prominent
California black artist. Tonee loved the piece and kept
setting it in different spots trying to find its proper
place. Tonee had a few small things to remember her
Ellen by. The new piece brought her joy and tears.

       Tonee's days were filled with the computer
always on her lap with the tv on mostly with Food
Channel. My days of watching lots of sports were
dwindling as Tonee took command of her space. She
found and printed lists of apartments for me to check.
I made a list of the major high end car dealers for
work. We even called a few landlords before I left.
The one that seemed most promising was in Kailua
on the windward side. Tonee was great on the phone.
She pronounced the landlord's name with a Germanic
accent. He was Swiss born. Tonee was able to speak
a little German with him. I got on the phone for a
moment to say hello. I told him I didn't speak German.

       Talking finances with Tonee was never easy.
She put in part of the projected security deposit and
first month's rent very reluctantly. She drove me to the
Hartford airport in strange silence. We hugged and
kissed. I was afraid of Mama having two weeks to
gain control. Tonee said she would stay in the

apartment with the pussycats. She would keep her same work and visit schedule with Mama, not letting her know I had left for Hawaii. She still did all the shopping and cleaning and laundry for Mama.

The flight out was a day of waste. I landed exhausted and went straight to the car rental. The cost was higher than expected. This trip was going to burn my budget. The feel of the hot sun and the cool trade winds calmed me some. I was uncomfortable in an unfamiliar car driving to the North Shore. I picked up some red wine and a Teds haupia and chocolate cream pie. The dogs met me at the gate. Their mouths were moving, but no sound came out. Ken had all his adult dogs debarked. It was a strange thing.

I rested for a day. The plan was to apartment hunt first. I figured the job search would be quicker. I called Tonee. She sounded like a little girl missing her Daddee. We went over her list of apartments. I missed her so much. I made some calls and had a few appointments lined up, two on the north shore and the other on the windward side in Kailua at the home of the Swiss. His name was Vern, short for Werner.

Tonee had sent me off with her portable navigation system. I couldn't get it to work. Lynette gave me pretty good directions for the north shore. I went to those the first day of looking, but did not like the look or feel of either. Lynette saw the begging on my face and offered to go with me to find the place in Kailua the following afternoon.

We left early going by Mapquest written directions. We missed the proper exit and backtracked, getting to Kailua an hour and a half early. We drove by the house which was barely visible from the street. It was built into the side of the hill. The car port was at street level. We recognized the house by the big red nautical buoy resting in front of the retaining wall at street level.

Lynette and I stopped for a burger, then found our way to Kailua Beach which was beautiful and long. The sand was softer than at the north shore and the water was calmer. I put my feet in the warm water and felt at home.

There was no ringer or bell at the gate to Vern's house. We yelled, but no one came. Finally, we opened the gate and walked down the dozen steep steps and yelled again. Vern came from behind the house, shirtless and sweating. He was in his sixties medium, stocky muscular build with grey hair, breathing hard having just returned from his run.

He was friendly and intelligent, showing us his property. He lived on the second floor. The rental was below him, space hollowed out from the hill. The apartment was large for Hawaii and sunny with lots of windows.

Vern asked some questions and gave us some history of his home of forty years and how he had built the lower apartment mostly by himself. He seemed to like me and Lynette was a great local reference. He said a young couple had put a deposit down last night after he had talked to me. He would call me if there was any change.

I was disappointed. I never liked apartment hunting. I had been hoping for early luck. The next morning, I started making calls again and set up a couple of stops for the following day. To my surprise, Vern called and said the apartment was available. The other couple had put a deposit down on a different apartment before seeing Vern's. That landlord would not give them the deposit back, so they asked Vern who cooperated with a refund.

Lynette came with me again because I was not comfortable with the directions.

Vern was surprisingly accomadating, taking one month's security deposit and first month's rent. He would hold the space through the month of June, doing a few improvements. I signed a one year lease, feeling a great relief. I thanked Lynette so much for her help. I called Tonee as soon as we got back. It was six hours later in Massachusetts. I wanted to get her before bed. She was surprised and said "good work." Then Tonee told me she had a second interview the next afternoon. She was excited.

That evening, the bigger Schnauzer had a litter of four puppies. Tonee was leaning towards a Schnauzer, but she wanted a female. All four were boys. They were so cute cuddling to their mother, their eyes not yet open.

It looked as if the move was a reality. Four days in and now I needed a job. I made my list of five high end dealers. Lynette showed me where they were in Honolulu on the map. The plan was to go to the Audi dealer first, then try the others. First thing in the morning, I called and spoke to the Audi Sales manager. He was interested since I had five years experience with the brand. I took my notes and the map and headed to Honolulu, circling and backtracking for an hour and a half, missing the Audi store and the others in the area. No one I asked could give clear directions. I had no cell phone and could not call Audi. I found the highway and headed back towards the airport, remembering the Infiniti Dealership I had seen earlier in the week. It was on my list.

I found The Infiniti Dealerlership, went in and asked to see a sales manager. I took a drink of water and waited. Ten minutes later, Mike appeared, a tall young Haoli guy with blonde hair and a friendly personality. He was the owner's son in law. We talked for ten minutes and then he said "You've got the job. When can you start."

I told him July 17, six and a half weeks out. He had a second manager meet me as protocol. Then I was introduced to Debby in HR to get paperwork started. She was delightful and went over benefits and pay plan and had me fill out all the papers. She said I would need a Driver's Abstract for my driving record and I'd have to get a sales license. This stuff was new to me. I took the paperwork for the license and abstract back with me.

Ken and Lynette were surprised at my immediate success. Lynette offered to go with me the following day for the abstract and license. It took a few hours the next day and Lynette and I brought the papers to Debby. She said they would do the background check and I would be set to work when I was ready. She said she would call if there was anything else she needed.

Mike said the background check was routine and unless I was a serial hatchet killer, there would be no problems. I didn't hear from Debby so I called her a few days later, checking in before I left.

"We're all set here. See you in July Robert."

I still had six days left. I called the airline. It would cost $100 to change the flight. The car rental was the same way. It was time for the beach. I came into the tv room that afternoon. Ken was doing his dance aerobics to the tv. It struck me funny and I laughed a little. That night,
Ken said he was used to his own space and asked me to rent a room till I left. There was a cheap place across from Pipeline, $75 night and no lock on the door. Chickens cackled all day and night in space

below the rooms. At dawn, a rooster went off right under my head. It was okay. I kind of enjoyed the freedom. I stopped back at Ken and Lynette's a couple of days later with a Ted's pie. I called Tonee and updated her. She was lonely. They took me out for Kahuku shrimp and we said Aloha till July. I took the flight back with little money in my pocket.

The long flights were awful. The last plane from Minneapolis to Hartford was a smaller commuter prop plane. The pilot aborted the first landing because of wind conditions. The second go around made me very nervous as I sat in the window seat behind the wings. As we approached the ground, the plane tilted wildly from side to side. I thought the wing was going to hit the ground. I thought the pilot would abort again, but he went in slamming and bouncing to a long halt. Everyone looked shook. The stewardesses and pilot wore the white faces of near death as I passed them to get the hell off that plane.

Tonee met me at the airport. We kissed and hugged. That last flight shook me up.

Tonee asked me all about my new job and the apartment. She seemed excited. Then she started on about her new job as sales manager for a crew of three at a nearby college. It was the sort of place that gave questionable degrees in IT and security or cosmetology or blood letting. The school was expensive, mostly drawing poor kids who had government grants and loans. Tonee said she had never been a manager before and didn't know how to get her crew to do better. Only one of the three met sales quota. It was so bad, Tonee would fill in and land recruit after recruit to keep the numbers up. The only thing she liked was the good pay check.

Tonee had Lynette update her on the puppy litters. Another batch of smaller Schnauzers was born.

We made an appointment to talk to Rabbi Edelman at his house. He was very nice and asked Tonee a bunch of questions. It became very obvious that the process of our having a completely kosher home to meet his standards would not work. Tonee would not lie. She said it wasn't that important to her to have a legal or religious marriage.

"God knows our love and our hearts. You are my husband."

Tonee had been seeing Carol, the Psychologist once a week. I drove her for the Wednesday night appointment after Tonee came home from work. They were getting along well. She had referred Tonee to a psychiatrist who prescribed her meds. I sat down with Carol for ten minutes privately. The one thing she said that was a surprise and I didn't understand was that most DID's sent in a pinch hitter for sex, a specialist so to speak. All of Tonee's personalities were Tonee. Carol said she met the six year old one night. They were almost done with a session. Apparently, Carol started whistling to herself as she was making notes. She heard a little voice.

"I don't like that. Stop whistling." Carol had woke a memory of Elinor's poor whistling. The little girl only stayed for a couple of minutes. "I have to go now."

Tonee liked Carol. I was afraid we might have a hard time getting Tonee a good person in Hawaii.

Our trip was four weeks away. We had to pack and throw things out. I was bad at paring down my belongings. We were both last minute procrastinators. Tonee kept up her job even though she hated it. The money was good. Management was beginning to pressure her for more performance.

Tonee would get up at 7:30 for work at nine. One morning as I lay in bed trying to sleep, I felt a little tap on my arm. I looked up to see Tonee all dressed for work, her shoulders slumped, crying, eye shadow melting into her face.

"I don't want to go to work. Do I have to Daddee?"

I was still groggy.

"Yes you do. But you can lay in bed with me first."

I took her hand and held it against my penis through the sheet. She looked horrified and pulled away and ran down the stairs. Then I realized she was just a little girl and I felt awful. I ran down after her and held her in my arms.

"It's okay sweetheart. I'm sorry. You can stay home all day if you want."

Tonee was a trooper. She cleaned her face, kissed me goodbye and went off to a day of hard sell.

The next few weeks were hard and combative. I came back from the last trip very tired and with a sore back. I started to filter my belongings, throwing out box after box of old business records. I had a mover set up. I went over rates and tried to figure as best I could how much spacial volume we could afford. They also tacked on fuel and mileage and weight surcharges.
Tonee had some things she had left with a friend in California that she wanted picked up on the way. The mover could do it at a cost. I kept telling Tonee we were okay, that we could afford it, that we would be fine in Hawaii with both of us working. The numbers were tight and I worried especially after the costs from my last trip.

Each Saturday, we would spend time at Tommy and Lisa's shop, sometimes buying a piece of furniture or art that wasn't in the budget. When I'm depressed, I like to shop. Tonee and I were like two little kids.

I asked Tonee to do the packing for the delicate things, like my Israeli pottery. She said she was a great packer, but she always put things off to the last minute.

Tommy knew a guy who had shipping boxes and wrapping stuff cheap. I asked Tommy if I could use a couple of his workers for a day to finish my move. Tommy said no, but he would do the job himself with his little truck for a moderate cost. I could not get him to be more specific. I asked him if he would buy some of my furniture since that was his business. He said he would stop by soon, but the prices would be very cheap.

I'd always thought that Tonee would be a healer for me. Lately, I was wondering if she might be my end. She kept pushing me to move things and pack. Some days, she would ask me if we could stay and not move. Tonee hadn't told her Mother yet that we were Aloha. We also needed to use space in her big garage for storage. The plan was to ship as much as we could afford and store the rest for a return visit home in a year or so. We could visit family and ship the balance out once we had money again. With one and a half weeks till the shippers arrived, the tension was terrible.

Tonee was still working five days a week and helping her Mama on Saturday. I was tossing things and packing some for storage. The delicate stuff was untouched. Tommy and Lisa came over one night, bringing us a home cooked meal. They were very nice. Tommy showed me how to pack Poppy. He looked at my furniture, much of it bought recently from him. He wouldn't put a price on anything. He said he didn't want to insult me.

We finished packing in the afternoon the day before the movers arrived. I made piles of boxes approximating what I thought would fit in our budget. I had hoped to be able to take some furniture, but that was looking bleak. I felt so stupid for some of the frivolous buying I had done recently. Tonee was still so angry at everything. We drank wine. I had my clipboard and sheets of paper with notes of what should go and what should be stored. We still had no place for storage and no help to move it. I hugged Tonee and asked her forgiveness for all the pressure.

"I love you Robert. I'd do anything for you."

"I love you Baby."

There was a corner with big boxes of kitchen stuff and a corner for my cd's and Israeli artifacts and a corner for Tonee clothes and things and a corner for mine. There was still so much that wouldn't go. I needed to step up and dump my clutter. I managed to clear a huge pile of stuff for the trash. It was a large apartment that I had filled. I had been through several big moves in my life. They were all well planned disasters.

The movers came late in the morning the next day. I showed the man what I wanted to ship. He took measurements and showed me an estimate double our budget. I had underestimated the extra charges and the stuff to be picked up in California and the dead space underneath the pallets and the cost and space of the huge shipping containers they provided. Tonee gave me a look of "I told you so asshole." My adrenalin was nasty. I wanted to puke. I stepped back and pared box after box and all the pictures. Tonee hadn't even packed some of her personal stuff. The movers took 41 boxes into the truck and I signed their paperwork in budget including California. There was so much that didn't go that should have and plenty that did go that should not have. I gave the man a check and sat out in the sun, sick of it all. I tried to do it right and it could have been worse, but it absolutely should have been better. I'd always been able to handle pressure, but it always took its eventual toll. I hated being dumb.

Tommy and Lisa brought dinner again. Tommy said to give him a call if I needed help with the rest. "Thanks Tommy." I liked him, but I didn't trust him.

The movers were gone. The apartment was clutter and chaos. Tonee looked scared and nervous. She promised to tell her mother that day about our move to Hawaii and to ask her for storage in the barn. I called John, my landlord, for help. He came over and agreed to help us move the storage stuff. He liked my pristine 1903 gas stove that came from my old house. He would take the stove in trade for his efforts. I told him he could also have some of my old furniture if he wanted.

Tonee came home after a day with Mama. She looked beat. She said her Mother wasn't surprised at the move. She agreed to let us use the room in the barn for storage. I gave Tonee a big hug.

John came over early the next day with his girlfriend. The three of us emptied the apartment into his truck. John was in charge with bull strength and a magician's mind at packing and space usage. I did more heavy lifting than I had done in a long time. We got most of it in one load and John directed a precision unload into our storage room. Everything was safe and accessible. We did one more half load and the storage began to lose its accessibility. I needed to finish the move with a lot of tossing for rubbish. John left at the end of the day with his old stove. He and his girl did a great job. I stopped for a minute in the craziness of the day to thank Mama for her help. She nodded her head in acknowledgement.

Our flight was in three days, the fourth of July. I asked Tonee if she had good suitcases. She said they were at Mama's. I tried to get the cats onto a flight to Hawaii two days in a row without success. There were new rules regarding air temperature and many airlines wouldn't take pets anymore. I found a contact with a big heart who agreed to take them, but I would have to get new, bigger shipping containers for my seventeen pound pussycats. Finding a pet store open on the fourth of July was a nightmare, but I found the containers and got the boys on board a separate airline from ours, two hours before we were to fly out.

Tonee had no suitcases. I went out the night before and bought her a big red one for the flight. She had an old clothes carrier and a piece of carryon luggage. It seemed she had lost one of her suitcases full of her summer belongings in the move from California.

The apartment was not as neat and clean as I would have preferred. Our bags were packed. Tonee's Uncle Dickie would drive us to the airport. Tonee was storing her car at his house until we could afford to ship it. I had sold my car to a wholesaler the day before.

An hour before we were to leave, Tonee asked me if she could stay for a while and make some money and then move out to meet me in Kailua. She was shaking. I hugged her and told her things would be okay.

"I'm scared Bobby. I feel like the time I flew to Arkansas to get married."

"We're gonna be good Baby. Hawaii will be healthy for us."

Uncle Dickie drove us to the airport. I got lost trying to find the right airline. I carried too many bags too many times that day. I was exhausted and angry and scared. I had never lived outside this area. Hawaii was a long way from everything.

Tonee asked again before we boarded our first flight if she could stay. She was a scared little girl. I just wanted to make her feel happy and protected. I thought I was doing the right thing.

"You're going to love Hawaii. We'll be happy there."

We boarded the first flight and left New England far behind. Tonee ordered a couple of drinks and then a couple more and started to relax, resting her head on my shoulder, to a needed sleep. What a beautiful woman. The plans and packing and lifting and getting the cats on their flight was over. I was stiff and sore and exhausted. The forward motion of the plane made this mad plan feel more genuine and correct.

ALOHA

The plan, after the full day of flights and airports was to go to Ken and Lynette's house for dinner and a good sleep. The next day,we would use their old Honda to drive back to the airport and pick up the cats who would be arriving in the late morning. They had stayed overnight in Houston in a pet hotel. I was worried about them.

Ken and Lynette were a little late at the airport. That gave me enough time to get really upset at the last airline for destroying one of my suitcases. Nobody seemed to care. It had been a horrible last flight. I was pissed off and sore. Tonee took it all in and let me let it out. I think I was venting for the whole moving process.

We ate good Thai food again, much needed and appreciated. It was dark when we arrived in Haleiwa. The dogs were barking silently. I left everything in the car except our carry ons. I helped Tonee up the rough slope to the house where she made a straight line for the puppies. Her face lit up. She played with everyone. Then, the litter of bigger Schnauzers took her full attention.

"Bobbie, I'm in love."

Her smile was enormous.

"Do you have a favorite?"

Tonee lifted her arms, showing me the biggest schnauzer of the lot. His markings were dark and beautiful. The little guy squirmed and nuzzeled into Tonee's warmth.

"Bobbie, he's so beautiful."

I took Ken aside and told him I had promised Tonee a puppy. If he would allow me payments, I wanted Tonee to go home with her new puppy. Ken gave me the you better follow through look and said okay. He gave me a price break. I asked him not to say anything to Tonee. It was starting to be a good day in Hawaii.

We sipped wine and watched a movie. The baby shnauzer slept in Tonee's lap. Tonee had a look of young, quiet contentment. She smiled and giggled till we went to bed, to sleep.

The next morning, we had breakfast. Tonee was holding the little, big schnauzer, a look of sadness that she would be leaving him soon.

"Too bad you don't like any of them." I kidded her.

"Bobbie, he's so amazing."

"Well, you're going to have to give him a name."

"What do you mean Bobbie?" Her eyes were looking at me in question.

"Welcome to Hawaii Tonee. I'd promised you a puppy dog. We're taking him home."

Tonee screamed and cried and hugged everyone. She wore a look of incredulous joy.

"Are you sure Bobbie?"

Ken set her up with a little box and some food and flea medicine. He started to talk to her about puppy care. I don't think Tonee heard a word or noticed anything but the little baby in her arms. She hugged Ken and Lynette.

"Thank you."

We headed to the airport to get the Honkers. Tonee's little baby slept in her lap the whole way. She had a grin of contentment.

The cats were ready to go when we arrived. They looked exhausted and very unhappy. The paperwork took a few minutes. Somehow, we made it home to Kailua getting lost only two times. The stress and fatigue pushed me to yell and scream. I put it all in a pocket when we arrived. I helped Tonee down the steps to our new home. I carried the luggage in three trips. Tonee looked around, carrying her baby.

"I like it."

I drove to the market down the street and brought a few essentials home. Vern came home from work after five. He hugged Tonee and gave me a "she's okay" wink. He loaned us a few chairs and an old mattress. I had bought an inflatable queen size plastic mattress, but Tonee figured we could save money and return it, so we set up borrowed sheets on the soiled lumpy old mattress. Lynette had loaned us linens and towels.

The cats had run and hid. Freddy was behind the stove and wouldn't even come out for food. Pita was bolder and checked around. He sniffed the little doggie, then jumped on my lap for comfort. I was worried that Fred would have trouble adjusting. Our shipment from the mainland was still 2-3 weeks out. The Beckers had arrived in Kailua. Tonee had her son. Except for the crazy jet lag and sore everything, it was a good day.

We ate Chinese at a nearby restaurant. Tonee

and I loved for the first time in our new home.

"Bobbie, I know I've made things difficult. It's not because I didn't want to come. I can't imagine life without you. You have given me the nicest gift I ever had. I never had my own doggie. I love you with all my heart and soul."

"I love you my Beauty. You make me happy."

Tonee got up off that lumpy old mattress and played for hours in the living room with her new baby boy, yet to be named.

"Tooki, tooki, tooki." She was a child on the floor in happy time. The little guy was barely the size of her hand.

Pita joined me on the old mattress, purring as I slept well for the first time in days. Tonee came to sleep much later, clutching her baby.

TV and internet and phone service were scheduled for the next day. Vern gave us his old TV and went out and bought himself a new one. Freddy had made his way to the food a couple of times, scrambling back behind the stove for safety. Vern took a liking to our puppy. He said he might want one of his own. It seemed like a great idea having the two to play with each other. Tonee was busy working on a dog name.

The next day, Vern drove us to the North Shore. He picked out the Schnauzer that was Tonee's second choice, a silver brother. Vern wanted to name him Freddy. I told him the name was taken. The new guy was "Wolfie."

Tonee had Wolfie in her lap all the way home. When we settled in, Vern left the new puppy with us. I brought him up to Vern and said they needed to take time bonding. A half hour later, Wolfie was wandering alone outside.

Vern set up a penned in area. It was half grass and half dirt with a little area for shade and rain protection. Tonee played with the little guys. When darkness came, our little guy came in. I asked Vern if he was going to have Wolfie in at night. He said no. Wolfie cried alone in the dark till we brought him in.

I had told my boss at Infiniti that I would start in two weeks. Tonee was considering starting her job sooner. We only had one borrowed car, so we'd have to work something out. We went to the beach. The water was great. Tonee went in, but was uncomfortable with the uneven surfaces and little pieces of seaweed floating in the water. She couldn't stand anything touching her that she couldn't see. She sat on the beach and calmed herself with cigarettes.

We visited Tommy in Kaneohe a couple of times. The care home was small. Everyone seemed very nice. All Tommy wanted to do was smoke. We took him to McDonalds. He loved his coffee. He had no teeth and barely chewed his food, sometimes coughing and choking, spitting his food onto the table. Tonee noticed an old gold ring with a cluster of red stones that Tommy wore. He offered it to her. Tonee said she would trade him the next time we visited.

We returned to see Tommy. Tonee had picked out four rings for the Flower to pick one or two for trade for his ring. Tony Flower's eyes went big and he put all four rings onto the fingers of his hands, some bleeding because the fit was too tight. Tonee didn't have the heart to ask for anything back.

I set us up with cell phones that would help us

stay in touch. They would also be necessary for work. On my phone, I set her name as Big Tonee. Her special ring tone was a dog barking so I knew it was my special love.

Tonee's son was named Kona. He got a little bigger and noisier each day. He and Wolfie were barkers, one setting the other off. Wolfie was getting no training. I was very worried for his future.

Tonee and I drove to parts of the Island she hadn't seen. She said other than the steep Koolau Mountains that ran through the center of the island, there wasn't anything better than what she had seen in California. We did see some great waterfalls, but Tonee was reluctant to hike very far to see some neat places. She was nervous about starting work and leaving her puppy unattended. The little guy was getting bigger each day and loved his Mommy. I liked the puppies, but I grew up with cats and my two honkers were my pet loves. Freddy and Pita began to relax and I let them outside a little. Whenever there was a new person on the property or a loud noise, Freddy went into hiding.

Tonee was in puppy heaven. The two were inseparable when she was home. Wolfie was like a lost orphan. Vern took him inside some, but mainly, Wolfie was totally alone when Kona was not with him. When it rained, he would crawl up against our window, soaked, until we let him in.

Tonee had no benefits at her job. In order for me to cover her for medical, we would have to be married. I kept pushing Tonee, because there was a time cutoff for the sign up. She absolutely had to have medical coverage. We knew we were going to be married anyways so why wait. Tonee looked into the paperwork for the state. She made contact with the Rabbi at the Synagogue off the Pali Highway. She had the state paperwork done and made an appointment for us to meet and talk to the Rabbi. To our surprise, he signed our paperwork and walked us outside on that sunny afternoon and married us in the shade of a beautiful palm tree. It was quick and kind of fun. We kissed and laughed, thanked the Rabbi, and left.

A few days later, Tonee came up to me and said she didn't think it would make a difference if we were married.

"But I was wrong Bobbie. It makes me feel real good to be your wife. I'm so proud. Thank you."

"I love you Tonee."

A week later, she came home with Jade wedding rings for both of us. I never wore jewelry, but I promised her that I would wear the ring.

Starting work was like leaving paradise, long hours and the stress of commission sales. We both operated on draw against commissions. My job had strong benefits, so we used my insurance. Mike, my boss, who hired me, showed me the less expensive used cars that were in good condition. I picked out an Infiniti to bring home to show Tonee. She drove it and loved it and called it Jade because of its color. My credit had a bankruptcy because of the failure of my business, but one local Credit Union gave me a loan with decent rates. I used the old Honda till Ken asked for it back, then I bought a used Honda with a second loan. Tonee seemed to like her job, using her navigation system to get around. She even used it in Kailua. I made some calls to the mainland, selling Tonee's Audi back to the dealership I worked at. I sent a check to Audi to clear up the balance.

I started to have problems with my back and left leg and knee. My Doctor kept sending me for physical therapy and massage which didn't solve the issue. I finally went to an orthopedic specialist who diagnosed bad hips in one minute. Xrays showed arthritic conditions in both hips with hip replacements somewhere in my future, to be put off as long as I could handle the discomfort. He recommended I sleep with a pillow between my legs. I needed to be careful with over exertion.

Vern said the neighbors were complaining about the dogs barking all day when we were gone. The bigger they got, the bigger the bark. The dog pen started to get nasty when it rained. The puppies always needed a bath. Vern constructed a temporary fence giving the dogs half the yard to run in. It was fun seeing their energy. At night, Wolfie slept near Vern's back door. He barked at any noise or stranger passing near the property. Vern didn't know how to deal with him other than to yell and spank him. I was beginning to worry that Wolfie would not have a good life. We bought some collars that would help control the barking. It worked okay for a while.

Tonee came home exhausted and tried to make dinner every night. She would drink a couple of bottles of wine and sneak smokes outside when Vern was not around or sleeping. She began to fall more often, sometimes outside when she was smoking and sometimes inside on the rug. I didn't know if it was her balance or the drinking, but she took some heavy hits. Fortunately, she had a rock hard head and never seemed to get badly hurt. It scared me to death. She would get angry when I suggested she drink less. With two pussycats and two puppy dogs around, I was afraid she would trip and fall more. I would lift her off the floor and she would have her quirky Tonee smile, like she just avoided death and it was no big deal. Tonee was a woman with more lives than a cat.

My work was okay. I liked most of the people around me. The hours were long. Some nights, I wouldn't get home till after nine. My sales were up and down, but I was top salesman two of my first five months. Some paychecks were good and some not. Tonee said things were good at her job, but her paychecks were always the flat draw. I tried to ask her about her record keeping for commissions, but she was angry whenever I asked. Paying bills, especially the rent was stressful. Vern was Swiss and set like a clock. Tonee would get upset and say I was keeping information from her and that she wouldn't support me. Sometimes she would give me money for bills without issue, but that was the exception. We were settling in and getting some used furniture and a new bed. Our stuff from the mainland had arrived. Tonee made the apartment into a home.

The mall was forwarded from Massachusetts. We started receiving collection notices from different sources for Tonee. She would get angry when I asked, but she needed my help and I did the best I could to settle some of her debts. The process would take time.

We had Vern over for dinner a couple of times. I would usually cook on the gas grill outside. He liked the dinners and was friendly and talkative. As usual, I had little to say. I had dealt with Vern a couple of times when we were a little late on the rent. He could be nasty. I began to enjoy his company less.

I got an email from Israel. My Mother had died. I had been praying for her passing. I hoped her soul would find peace again. I took a week off from work in observance. I was tired. Tonee was upset at my time away from work.

Tonee kept in touch with her Mother. She showed me letters where Mama was saying good things about me. One day, we received via UPS, a beautiful hand crocheted Afghan from Mama for Tonee. I encouraged Tonee to call often and stay in touch with her Mother. Sometimes, Tonee would cry missing her.

Tonee was always online with the computer in her lap and the tv on. She was always looking for her next job. The Yellow Pages Oahu campaign would end soon. Unless she wanted to fly to Maui, there would be no work till next year. Tonee had worked at the L.A. Times for a little while and she kept talking about a sales job with one of the two newspapers. She interviewed at both and came home excited one day that she had a second interview scheduled at the Aloha Bulletin, the smaller of the two papers. She dressed up, went in, and got the job with a strong salary plus commissions. She would start in two weeks. She came home excited and a little scared.

I was happy for and proud of her. She said she was a great interview. Her current employer had been promising her commissions. I offered to get involved. She said not yet. One night, she came home late, having to chase people down to give her some more money. She came home with a check that would cover a full month's rent. They promised her a little more money when their clients paid. Tonee cleaned up her business with the Yellow Pages, taking a few days off to chill.

The night before she started her new job, we were sitting quietly in the living room. She half stood up and fell slamming her head badly on the wood coffee table. I started to get up to help her as her head slammed down a second time even harder before I could reach her. She fell back on the floor crying and holding her hands to her face. I had never seen anything like that in my life. I didn't know how it happened or why, but I couldn't stop her before she hurt herself. She had fallen so many times before, but this was bizarre. Her lip was bleeding and her face was swollen. Both eyes were puffing and bruised. I helped her to the couch and held her. She looked at me like a little girl, so badly hurt. This world was hard on Tonee. She did not want to go to the hospital. I put some ice in a bag and she held it to her face.

"What happened Bobbie?"

"I don't know."

All night long, she tossed in bed, kicking with her feet, mumbling and talking, but I couldn't make out words. In the morning, she insisted on going to her new job. Her eyes were black and blue and her lip swollen. I drove her to her new job. I kept asking her to call in sick. She wouldn't let me help her further. She was all dressed to kill, but she looked like someone beat her to it. I told her to call me when she was ready to go home.

She made quite an impression the first day. They thought I had beaten her, but Tonee told them no. She was driven to a doctor's office who cleaned her up and gave her a catscan and some medicine for the swelling and pain. She had some damage to her right eye that would take time to heal. Tonee had arrived in style at the Honolulu Aloha Bulletin. It would be quite a relationship. Tonee called me in the late afternoon and I drove her home. My precious baby was in need of care and some puppy love.

With recommendations from co workers, we set up with personal doctors and a dentist. Tonee had been using a Psychiatrist in Honolulu who she described as a cold bitch. Tonee didn't like our first family doctor, so she found another. When the Doctor checked out her mouth, she thought there were sores in her mouth that might be cancer and Tonee needed to see a Dentist for clarification now. Getting Tonee to a Dentist was difficult. She was scared to death of dentists, but the cancer scared her more. She admitted to a lot of pain in her mouth.

Her first appointment with Dr. Mark, the dentist, was a huge cry fest. I finally got her in the car and to his office.

"I'm scared Bobbie. What if it's cancer?"

"I'm sure it isn't. Don't worry. You're gonna be great. I won't let anyone hurt you."

An hour later, Tonee came out with Dr. Mark following. She looked like a six year old who had been spanked. Dr. Mark looked worn. He said there was no cancer, just a lot of infection. Tonee would need a lot of work on her gums and teeth. We scheduled the next appointment for a deep gum cleaning two weeks out. Tonee received a prescription for antibiotics. The odyssey of her mouth had just begun.

Tonee had talked before about her history of eating disorders from when she was a teenager on. She'd been bulemic and anorexic with the toxic effect destroying the health of her gums and teeth and gave her acid reflux. Tonee cried and said she had something to tell me that she'd always been afraid to say.

"My lower teeth are all dentures except for the

front three. I was afraid to tell you. Are you angry Bobbie?"

"I love you Baby. You are my beautiful little girl. We're going to get you healthy. I can't be angry with you."

I will admit it caught me by surprise, but life with Tonee was a cycle of surprises and change. We had some wine and watched a comedy on tv.

A week later, Tonee said she was worried about her Mother. Her voice had been hoarse for a while. She said she was going to a Doctor to check it out. Then she mentioned that little Ziggy went off one night to sleep and hide in the closet, to pass. Tonee shook and cried.

The following month, Mama was admitted to the hospital with cancer of the jaw. She said the prognosis was good and that Tonee shouldn't come to visit. Tonee cried and cried. It couldn't be good. Her Mother was in her eighties.

Tonee lit candles at home each night and prayed. Her step sister called and gave her the heads up that her Mother wouldn't make it. Two weeks later, Jackie was in the ground. Tonee seemed kind of numb. I felt bad for having separated them.

Tonee went to work and acted okay, but I thought I saw a week or two of dead eyes.

The puppy dogs were getting much bigger and their hair was shaggy dog look. Vern and I took the two guys to the groomer. I didn't recognize them when we returned. They were two handsome dudes. Tonee had hundreds of pictures of Kona. Her camera went crazy when she saw the newest Kona look.

I didn't know that would be the only time Vern would take Wolfie to the groomer. He looked great.

Vern even let him in his kitchen for a while that night.

My work was okay, just long hours and the life of up and down success. Overall, I was one of the top salesmen, but we always seemed an extra paycheck from comfort. Tonee's face and eye healed after her grand entrance to the new job. She settled in, but was soon complaining that her top boss was a misogynist bully. The bosses were all fucking their secretaries there.

She had problems with the floor where she worked, something about how smooth it was or the types of tiles and lines. She said getting up and walking that floor made the trip to the ladies' room an adventure. She went in every day and told me her sales were good. She was doing mostly in house phone sales, so there was not the worry of her walking too much. I still had a pile of parking tickets I found stuffed in her glove box from her last job. Tonee wouldn't quit. They changed her job a few times. She showed up and did her work.

Tonee had smoked for forty years. She'd tried to quit in years past. There was a pill that her Doctor recommended that would make her sick from both ends if she smoked. She tried it and went back to smoking. Now, she tried a second time and stuck with it. I had to clean vomit from inside her car as she got sick driving to work. For the first time in years, she could taste her food, not that it made her eat much more.

"You know Bobbie, most of my life, I didn't care if I lived or died. Now, I want to be healthy and have a long life with you and Kona. You're the first person in my life that I've truly loved."

"I'm so proud of you Baby."

One day, she came back from work with a big

stain in her ass. She had gotten sick, but wouldn't leave work. She had been written up many times and was afraid of getting fired.

Her behavior at home was often angry. She'd come home from work, exhausted and pissed off. She'd fly into rants that could go from room to room. Sometimes, she would attack me physically on top of the verbal abuse. I would just try to hold her and calm her down. Her mood could change at any time, up or down. When I went to bed, I wondered who would wake up next to me. The Bad Tonees were far too stressed. My little girls were tired and scared. All I could do was hang on and love her.

I'd become a Salvation Army and Goodwill addict, stopping at the stores each week, looking for little gifts for Tonee. The house was already filled with little angels and things that I bought hoping she would enjoy. She kept telling me not to bring anything else home, but I loved the look of surprise when she got something she liked. One morning I came home to Tonee, still in bed, with a crazy, funky paper machet toy that I almost left behind; Croc Daddy, a violet crocodile car on wheels with a green crocodile man waving from his car seat. The three year old smiled and grabbed Croc Daddy and whooshed him along the bed on his wheels, so alive and happy. "Whoosh, whoosh, whooosh.Thankee Daddee."

All through this time, Kona had grown into a doggie, so in love with his mother. He'd sleep at night on the pillow above her head. Tonee would sing and talk baby story to Kona. She had a language for the two of them. They were inseparable.

"tooki tooki"

"Sachi malli bunga"

Through all this shit at work was love.

"I want to be healthy for you Bobby. You and Kona are my life. I want us together forever."

We finally found a psychologist and a shrink in Kailua for Tonee. She went once a week to the psychologist, Rita, and once a month to the shrink for meds. Rita's approach was to live in the now. I think she had a grounding effect on Tonee. Tonee hoped they could be friends. She kept trying to find her Ellen in Hawaii. Rita was becoming the closest. The shrink started to cut Tonee's meds back.

Tonee went for several sessions at the Dentist's office. Her mouth was less sore. The next stop was to work with a gum and denture specialist. Tonee kept talking about the cost. All I wanted was for her to be healthy and happy and loving me. I didn't need anything else. We would find a way.

"I love you Bobbie. Do you love me? I don't want you to be mad at Tonee. I have some big news."

Tonee called me at work one day, so happy and light. She'd been fired from the Aloha Bulletin after a year and a half of hell. The world of shit she had been working in was gone. She would collect unemployment and stay home and chill for a while if I had my way.

In the early stages with Rita, I would always bring Tonee in. She had a bad history with appointments on her own. I met and talked to Rita several times. I met Dr T. her shrink. I liked them both.

Tonee's manic episodes at home became much less frequent. Tonee would play with her doggee and watch Food Channel on tv and peruse the internet non stop with an emphasis on Ebay. Tonee loved to shop online. She'd always tell me things were just a dollar or two. Every six months, she'd have bags full of clothing and things for the Salvation Army.

Tonee had developed her collection of Schnauzer stuff; socks and shirts and jewelry. Each year she made a new Kona calendar with twelve special pictures.

Tonee had a history of destroying computers. Usually it would be computer viruses. She was using my old laptop, her third in three years. One night Kona jumped up and knocked a few letters off the keyboard. One of the little six year olds took some glue at midnight and put the letters back on. In the morning the letters were stuck solid. The entire screen was covered in glue. Time for a new machine.

Wolfie was getting sick. He lived outside. He was under fed and malnourished. I took Wolfie to the vet on my dime. He had mange. I started to bathe him more regularly and put some ointment on his sores. His hair began to grow in, but discolored. I had Vern hold Wolfie while I groomed him with electric shears that Ken had given me when he moved to Aica and sold his breeding business. I did a good job except I couldn't get near his face. Vern was caught by Wolfie's paws fighting his control, scratching him on the face and arm.

Later in the day, I knocked on Vern's door and asked him if I could take control of Wolfie, including feeding.

Vern agreed. The next day, he came down with a letter for me to sign outlining Vern's continued ownership of Wolfie. He did state that he would pay for Vet and Groomer appointments. I continued to feed and bathe him and the occasional shearing with Tonee's help. Washing Kona and Wolfie on the same day was good exercise. Wolfie slept near the back stairs to Vern's apartment on a pillow I gave him. That damn dog loved Vern despite his ill treatment. He craved attention, delighting in petsies when Tonee or I reached out. Wolfie would bark early in the morning and late at night, upsetting Vern's quiet. He had never been properly socialized.

When the fireworks went off on holidays and when it rained so heavily, Wolfie would shiver outside our window till we let him in. Tonee would towel him dry and hold him on her lap till Kona couldn't take it anymore. Wolfie would not be allowed to sleep in our bedroom with Kona. In the morning, there was usually pee and a poop in the kitchen. It was time to get his lion mane tamed. I made an appointment with the Vet for his checkup and shots that were long overdue and were mandatory for the Grooming appointment I had made. I went to Vern and told him I had the appointments set. Vern turned red and yelled at me telling me it was not my business and to leave his dog alone.

The next day, I went looking for Wolfie, but he was not around. I knocked on Vern's door and he told me he had given Wolfie to a friend. I went and told Tonee. She talked to Vern later in the day and he told her he brought Wolfie to the Humane Society. Wolfie was gone. What a shame. Fucking Vern.

Kona would go outside several times and look around and sniff for Wolfie. His Brother and playmate was gone. Tonee cried all day. There was an emptiness to the land around us. Home was less complete. It was a while till I talked to Vern again.

Tonee enjoyed her time off and the pleasure of not dealing with her former bosses again. She began to get bored and was worried that her collecting was not enough income. She'd send out resumes online. If she had an interview outside of Kailua, I would usually bring her. She did land a job at a temp agency in Honolulu that lasted a few weeks. Tonee didn't like the commute for the pay that was not much more than her collecting.

Freddie got sick. He stopped eating and drinking and hid in my closet most of the time. I tried to get him to eat and drink with some of his favorite treats. One week became several. I loved that big fat gray cat so much. We finally brought him to the vet. Dr. Zane said it was probably fatty liver disease which used to be completely fatal, but a technique had been discovered to force food and water into him. In twenty five percent of the cases, the cat would survive and begin to eat again. Freddie was on the verge of death. He said they would need to do bloodwork and could start the feeding if Freddie stayed overnight. He estimated the cost at five hundred dollars. Tonee and I talked and she said it was my decision. Freddie stayed for three days and was force fed. We could get the special diet food and do it at home. The bill was two thousand dollars, blowing us away. I was very upset, but I just wanted to get Freddie home and healthy. I could talk to them another day about the bill. I gave them five hundred dollars and Freddie came home.

I was scared to force the food into him. Tonee set up her station on the dining room table where she mixed the formula and medicine. I helped keep Freddie in place. Tonee put the tube in his mouth and little by little forced him to eat and drink. Freddie was gentle as always. Sometimes he would vomit mixture on Tonee or the carpet.

The vet called me a couple of times and

begged us to keep it up. He told of his old cat who went through the same thing and got a couple of more years from it. I admired Tonee's touch and willingness to do the work. The feeding went on for two more weeks till one day, he pulled up to Pita's water dish and drank on his own. He began to eat and his energy and weight increased. My Freddie was coming back to me. Bless Tonee for her wonderful efforts.

Tonee had been talking about getting another puppy or kitten for herself. She didn't think Kona would allow a dog, but he might put up with another cat. I didn't know how Fred and Pita would deal with it, but I couldn't deny Tonee, especially after her heroic work. She wanted a shelter cat. I promised her we would go one day.

Tonee did get one other job in Kaneohe eight miles away, working for a company selling vacation rentals online and on the phone. Tonee had a week of training where she couldn't take phone calls. When I did call her, I heard the ten year old, very serious and intent telling me I shouldn't call. She hated the computers and had great difficulty learning their system. She started selling and thought she was doing a great job, but they fired her after three weeks. She had misunderstood the pay plan and got a tenth of what she expected in commissions. Tonee left there disturbed and deflated.

Her energy seemed less than usual. She still kept applying for jobs, but nothing worked out. She began sleeping in later and going to bed late. Except for Kona and myself, she was alone. She and Vern seemed to get along okay, despite the Wolfie episode. The extension on unemployment was going to expire in a few months. I asked her if she would consider applying for Disability. I had talked to Rita about it and she thought it would be a good thing.

Neither of us thought Tonee was able to hold a full time job and maintain her health. After a while, Tonee started to think it might be a good thing not having to work everyday. Rita and Dr. T filled out their portions of the application. I made a written statement and Tonee did the rest.

Social Security Disability applications could take years. I went in with Tonee for her interview. We received an approval letter in six weeks. She would receive monthly benefits as well as a check backdating her disability to the end of her Aloha Bulletin employment. It was a wonderful thing. Tonee was delighted, but embarrassed by the process of having to show her basic incompetence. My beautiful woman was so intelligent and good hearted. Her special issues were a godsend and a curse.

To celebrate, we went to the Humane Society. Tonee fell in love with a golden tiger kitten, probably two months old. He seemed to have a friendly and comfortable nature. Ninety eight dollars later, we had another cat. His name was Dexter.

Freddie was getting back to his old nature. He was eating okay and even jumping on the bed to sleep near my head once in a while till Dexter jumped up on the bed next to him. Dexter was very vocal and liked to go outside. He was destroying our couch and would claw the screen door till we let him out. Sometimes, he would start meowing outside in the middle of the night till we let him in. I liked the guy a lot, but he was a handful. Tonee started to complain about his loud meowing. She enjoyed snuggling with him and Kona was moderately accepting. She started talking about sending him back. I couldn't imagine that. He was months older and it would be harder to find a home for him. I tried to calm Tonee down, but she was very sensitive to too much noise.

Freddie took a bad slide in his recovery. He stopped drinking and eating almost completely. It shook me up badly. I couldn't imagine force feeding him again. It was time to pray for Freddie and enjoy him while he was alive. After a week, he had a seizure, clawing and screaming. I held him on my lap for hours as he slept. I placed him on the couch. A week later, he was gone, my beautiful Freddie. I buried him in an open spot near the house, but not on Vern's property. I loved that beautiful spirit and now he was dead.

Some shit happened and I left Infiniti for the Acura Dealership on Ala Moana. It took me a while to get on track there. My poor income created stress and tension.

The work on Tonee's mouth was progressing. Insurance covered most of the work on her gums, but would not cover the dentures in her lower mouth. Her gums were healthier now, but her lower old denture was uncomfortable and ineffective for proper eating. The work would be the cost of a small car. We would handle it somehow. I talked Tonee into proceeding.

Tonee had been a trooper through all the work on her mouth. The morning she went in to the Oral Surgeon to have her remaining lower teeth yanked was a horror. Tonee didn't want to give up her last bottom teeth, but finally gave in to strong advice from Dr Mark and the Oral Surgeon. She came out of the back room after an hour and a half with a towel over her mouth, crying and shaking with the look of terror on her child's face. I helped her to the elevator and my car and drove to Dr. Mark's for the first denture fitting. It took another hour in Tonee hell. She came out exhausted and terrified. All I could do was get her home and hold her hand and open bottles of chilled white wine. It would take a few weeks for her mouth to heal and go in for the next fitting.

A month later, Tonee had a new smile and was so surprised at how well the dentures fit and worked. She ate and talked with comfort. The occasional whistle was gone from her voice. The horror of the dental work was in the past. I was so proud of her.

Her upper teeth were rickety, but would not be an active subject for a while.

Dexter was driving her crazy. She said he would have to go back. I didn't want to do it. She said the noise bothered her so much she might hurt him one day. I finally consented. I really liked the guy who was almost full grown now. I put him in the cage. He meowed all the way. When I brought him into the facility, he freaked. I opened the cage and tried to hold him for comfort, but he was wild with terror and scratched me till I put him back. I really hoped he could find a good home. So long Dexter.

Tonee settled into her life of not working, tv, computer, ebay and errands in Kailua which was home, even if she still didn't like Hawaii. She still had no best friend. She saw Rita once a week. Dr T had weaned her off meds. Tonee was in a calm. She had her Kona. That dog was spoiled crazy, but he was a good guy. Tonee still struggled with the stairs to the street and her car. We had talked of moving and Tonee was always looking online for apartments in Kailua, but we had a pretty good deal with Vern, despite his eccentricities. Tonee had a routine of walking Kona daily to build up her strength and clear her mind from spending so much time in the apartment.

One day, just before I was leaving for my afternoon shift, I received a call from a neighbor down the street. Tonee had fallen and needed help. I ran to my car. Kona was in the driveway, the leash trailing behind him, all excited. I brought him downstairs, then drove a block and a half to where Tonee lay in the side of the street.

Tonee had been walking Kona. A woman was walking her dog on the other side of the street. Kona lunged at her dog, wrapping the leash around Tonee's legs, bringing her down.

"I fell down, went Boom. It hurts so much Bobbie."

I thanked our neighbor. He helped me lift Tonee. She was in a lot of pain on her left side. I drove her home. I asked her if she wanted to see a Doctor. She told me to bring her to the hospital. Tonee could take a lot of pain. Something was very wrong.

Tonee had broken her left hip and wrist. Surgery on the hip would be the next day. The orthopedic Surgeon on call was from the clinic I used for my hips. He was not a hip specialist, but had a strong reputation. The nurses said we were lucky to get him. The Doctor explained that it would be a double surgery with the removal of the old titanium rod in her upper thigh from her broken leg a decade before. A plate would be put in to support the hip. He had to research and call the California hospital to find out what kind of screws and pins were holding it together so he would have the proper tools for removal. The wrist would heal naturally in an open cast. Tonee would need a few weeks at a rehab facility till she could properly get on her feet and handle steps. Tonee looked grim, but faced surgery without drama. All she asked for was enough medication to keep her pain tolerable.

The surgeon called me the following afternoon. The surgery had gone well. Tonee would be in post op for a couple of hours. I was waiting in her room when they finally wheeled her in. She was pale and exhausted. I kissed her lightly. She was still out there, mumbling about Daddy and wanting to play in the back yard. I stayed with her till she nodded off.

She would spend three days at the hospital before being transferred to a rehab center in Honolulu. The nurses asked me about her Daddy. I told them she got a little loopy with the medication. Tonee was giving them a hard time about her food. As wonderful a woman as she was, she was a tough patient. She could be angry and nasty. Tonee was full of fight.

The Doctor overseeing her at Castle was an acquaintance of mine. I had sold him a car. He kept telling her and me that her drinking was having a negative effect on her body and it was showing up in her blood work. I told him I tried to get her to ease off, but she was a stubborn woman who liked her drink.

They started to get her on her feet almost immediately at the rehab facility. She would walk to a chair in the room and sit down and stand up. They were getting her set to use a walker, but it was a little more difficult because she could not put pressure on her left wrist yet.

Tonee was worried about the bills and the dog and the cat and me. I told her everybody was fine and that her medicare A would help with the billing in addition to my coverage at work. Over the next week or two, her strength grew. She loved the people teaching her. She said she was already working on climbing steps.

My life was work, taking care of the animals and stopping in to see Tonee at least once a day.

Tonee's mood was up and down. Some days she was happy to see me and upbeat on her rehab and some days she was angry at everyone.

Kona and I went through a bonding. I appreciated his company. Pita slept at my feet and Kona on Tonee's pillow by my side. I offered to bring Kona in where there was a lawn downstairs. Tonee was afraid Kona would be too excited and could hurt her.

A few days before Tonee would come home, I went to rehab in the morning and watched Tonee go through her training. She was especially proud of her stair climbing. They showed me how to help her in and out of the car.

Tonee was ecstatic to be home. She was disappointed at Kona's reaction, almost as if the little guy thought she had abandoned him. A couple of biscuits later, Kona was a mama's boy again.

Castle Hospital in Kailua sent people to the house to evaluate how well Tonee could get around with the bathroom and especially the stairs leading up and out of the house. I bought her a specialty chair for the tub so she could shower. She received in house rehab three times a week and attacked it with fervor. After a couple of weeks, we were able to help her up the steps so she could get out of the house. Tonee wanted her independence. We had to jump start her car to get her going. She began to do rehab at a facility near the house. There were classes available through the YMCA for swimming and workouts which Tonee signed up for. She really liked her workout instructor at the Y and hoped they could be friends. Tonee was getting strong, almost buff. One day, she was all excited. She had made a new friend at swimming, Linda. Linda was there to help her husband, Dan, who had a stroke the prior year. They began to spend time together. Tonee would go to their house and work out in their little pool. She even went to weekly art lessons at the Honolulu rehab with Dan. Tonee worked on a painting of Kona. They were very grateful for Tonee's driving him each week. It took a load off Linda. Tonee was eating better. She had a girlfriend.

Her recovery from the surgery was like the birth of an amazon. She bought a used exercise bike and some other contraption on Craig's list. She was excessive in her working out. She really began to look strong and good. Her legs were no longer little sticks, but muscular all the way into her buttocks. My woman almost had an ass.

One day, I got a call from Kenneth. Tommy was at Castle Hospital, bleeding internally. They thought it was a burst aneurism in a main artery to his heart. They didn't expect him to survive. I called Tonee and left work to pick her up. We were at emergency before Ken and Lynette arrived. Tommy was semi conscious. The Doctor explained that surgery would be intense and the possibility of his surviving without severe brain damage was poor. Tonee and I agreed with Kenneth who would arrive soon. Tommy was dying. There would be no surgery. My oldest Brother, the gentle one; it was the day to say goodbye to his beautiful soul. He had lived a life we would call hell. He almost always was cheerful when we saw him.

Tommy was transferred to a large room on the second floor with a great view of the mountains. One of the nurses helped us understand the process, explaining it would take a few hours, and that he would lose his senses slowly. His pain would be properly managed. The last senses lost were sound and touch. I kissed my Brother and held his hand as he passed away. Tonee held his other hand and caressed his head. His face was toothless, but his skin was smooth and soft, almost young. There was an awful beauty to that afternoon. I felt blessed to be able to say goodbye.

It was a year since Tonee's Mother had died. Tonee's step sister, Jackie, was pressing us to get the storage room emptied so the house could be shown for sale. Tonee was ready to have everything taken by the Salvation Army. I called Tommy from the antique shop to see if he could help. A week later, the place was empty. Tommy tossed most of the stuff. I gave him a list of things I needed shipped to us. We would work out a deal for the things he would keep for his efforts. Tommy said he would call back with a cost. The Tommy ordeal had begun. He never gave me numbers or how he valued the things he would keep. We still had Tonee's grandmother's china and her family pictures and her beautiful bronze, Poppy. I had my cd collection and a couple of paintings from the family, One little picture was done by my brother, Tommy, when he was in the sixth grade. It was a beautiful, creative work. The stuff ended up in a storage facility.

Tonee was enjoying herself more, but she still didn't like Hawaii. She was always at the library getting new books to read and looking for new projects to start. She liked the people of Hawaii. She knew everyone at all the stores by name. She had a best friend. The only time she went near the ocean was when I would go and she would take Kona for a walk. She complained about the high cost of everything. She hated the bugs, but she loved the gheccos, letting them roam the house freely. When Tonee was angry, she'd pull out internet apartment listings for Philadelphia for herself and Kona.

We began to see Ken and Lynette more. Tonee always wanted to be close friends with Lynette, but now, she was even starting to like my Brother. Mostly, we'd go out to dinner. Sometimes, Tonee went on day trips with them to Chinatown or the North Shore.

Tonee started to hate her Infiniti, insisting she never liked Jade and I never gave her a choice. She wanted a coupe for the looks. I worked at Acura and suggested the RSX. We went and test drove one and she loved it. We found a good deal on Craig's List. Tonee was able to get her own loan through my Credit Union. She loved her new black on black coupe. She called it Raven.

Over the next year, Tonee and Linda drifted apart a little, to Tonee's great distress. Linda was spending all her time training to be a Life Coach. She kept trying to get Tonee to sign up.

The Audi Dealership moved from their lousy location to a large building and lot across the street from Infiniti. I had sold Audi for five years on the mainland. I went to Audi and got the job, leaving Acura after one and a half years, making better money almost from the start. The managers gave me a hard time initially, but I kept selling cars. The management kept changing and I had to get used to each regime. Tonee was always happier when I made money. I just wished I could always do the best. All I ever wanted was to make all her little girls and her big girls happy and at peace. Despite our ups and downs, there was no question of the love between us. Tonee called me her Husband with pride and adoration.

Tonee continued to see Rita. I think she had a

good way of planting Tonee on the present universe. I had become more familiar with Tonee's personalities and their intonations. Sometimes, I would ask to speak to one of the little girls and a little voice would come out so sweet and gentle. Once, I asked to speak to the three year old and was told it was too late. The little girl was already asleep. When I did hear that little tiny voice, she was like a little piece of candy, incredibly nice. Even the angry girls were starting to trust me more and weren't as vicious. She hadn't been violent since her early days with the Aloha Bulletin. Mostly, however, Tonee didn't like to talk much about her DID or the committee. I think the static voices in her head were calmer than years back.

Tonee started to slack off on her exercising and wasn't eating as well. She started to see a Kidney Specialist because her count was down. Her staple diet was gummee bears and girl scout cookies and Pennsylvania big Pretzels, heated and topped with whiz cheese. She over used salt. She still wanted to smoke but didn't. Sometimes, she would get angry at me for limiting her to wine instead of Vodka. I hadn't drunk anything when Tonee was in the hospital, but I got back into it when she returned home. Tonee still outdrank me two to one. She never had a hangover. I tried to get her to cut back, but that only made her angry. I never saw her staggering drunk from wine. She was falling less, but it scared me so much since she broke her hip. Her right knee was getting sore, supporting more since her injury. Sometimes, she'd lose her balance and sometimes, it looked like she just sort of lost it for a moment and fell. The joke was it was okay as long as she landed on her head. That woman had a helmet that could take a hit. She had a new woman doctor who sent her out for an MRI of her head. The results came back fine. She started on new supplements to help her bones and her kidneys.

Sometimes, Tonee would get angry at me and say I was more of a caretaker for her than husband. I did my best to protect her. I loved her so much. I couldn't stand it if she was badly hurt again. It was difficult to separate the little girls from the adults. Our lovemaking was less frequent than before her broken hip.

I still couldn't get completely used to her on off switch when I would be the biggest asshole in the world and ten minutes later, I was Bobbie again and she was in mucho love. Some of her tirades were repetitive messages, about money or living in Hawaii or my quiet personality. She called me her mute. My argument was when I did say something, she either didn't listen or just took it the wrong way and got angry. Tonee always had a fast mad button. Sometimes, when I'd look at her and say you were so mad at me five minutes ago, she'd just laugh and say "Do you want it to be easy?" Sometimes, we'd talk, and whoever I was talking to, an hour later, she didn't remember. I don't know how she functioned at work all those years, but I think her worker girl button was intense and capable. My beautiful woman was a survivor with style.

My beautiful white pussycat, Pita, started to get sick a year after his brother died. He was urinating constantly. He was diagnosed with Diabetes. I never knew cats got that disease. Both of my cats became ill from obesity. I wished I had dealt differently with their diets years back. Pita was sixteen. The insulin was expensive and he had to be monitored regularly. I wasn't comfortable giving him his shots, so my wonderful woman took over again to try to heal my big baby. Pita lasted about six months. We were never able to fully stabilize his condition. The night he died, I lay with him on the kitchen floor, finally falling asleep by his side. He was gone in the morning. I buried him in a slot of ground beyond the property zone of Vern. I was out of pussycats. I missed them both so much.

Tonee was complaining about her general sluggishness. I was worried that she was getting much weaker than she had been before she broke her hip. I watched her everytime she stood to walk in case I could keep her from falling. She began to complain about her left foot hurting. I asked her to use a cane for support. She refused. Getting up and down the stairs outside was painful and dangerous. She would hold the railing with one hand and touch the wall of the garage with the other for support. I was worried Kona would trip her up the stairs. I urged Tonee to see a Doctor for her foot and her general health. Her leg was swollen and leaking a clear fluid. She kept putting it off.
"I'm sick of Doctors. Leave me alone."
She finally went to an Orthopedic Specialist who couldn't find anything wrong with her foot. I was angry. I knew she was getting worse. She could barely walk. Her pain was intense. Over the next week, the pain in her foot became extreme. I made some calls and found an almost new wheelchair at the Salvation Army. Tonee was very appreciative and used it to get around the house. She could not get up the stairs to drive herself, so she was limited to my schedule for shopping. I insisted she get another visit to the Orthopedist. We went back a second time. The Doctor was shocked when the new xrays showed a crushed heel, the type of injury that would come from a fall off a three story building. The Doctor insisted the

injury was not there the week before. The only thing Tonee could vaguely remember was she might have tripped over Kona in the bathroom one night. It was an odd and mysterious and nasty occurrence.

She was referred to a foot specialist who looked at the xrays and told Tonee she might have cancer. I was not in the room at Tonee's insistence. She came out crying, asking me to talk to the Doctor. I went back in and the Doctor said there were a couple of specks in the heel xray that could be cancer. They would do more tests. Tonee was terrified. I tried not to overreact and calmed her down. The foot doctor was fighting a cancer of his own.

Tonee went for Cat Scans and an MRI. A week later, the results came back negative for cancer. We celebrated with a nice dinner out. I wanted my Tonee with me forever. She was so relieved. I felt better, like the survivor of a train wreck. I was exhausted.

Tonee would be off her feet until the heel healed naturally. Tonee was upset and depressed. The Doctors kept telling her to stop drinking or to slow down, but Tonee would not. I would bring the bottle to fill her glass. She'd get upset when I tried to moderate her usage. I was doing all the shopping and cooking and cleaning up. I didn't want anything to hurt my Baby. I offered to help her in the bathroom, but she refused. I had to set up the bedroom to accommodate the wheelchair. In the evening, I would help her into bed.

She was barely eating and wasn't drinking enough non alcoholic fluids. She began to look sickly. She broke a couple of wine glasses within a couple of days. I came home from work one night and she had dropped a bottle of wine. I cleaned up the broken glass and sticky wine from the carpet and floor. She couldn't hold a glass without dropping it. I held a water glass in my hand and had her sip through a straw. She was becoming angry and confused in a paranoid way. She needed to pee. I wheeled her to the bathroom and tried to help her pivot to the seat. She resisted and accused me of trying to hurt her. Sitting on the toilet, she asked for a sip of water. The glass slipped from her hand, shattering on the floor. I was so tired, I screamed and told her not to stand up till I picked up the broken glass. She asked me why was I trying to kill her. I told Tonee we should go to the hospital. She refused.

I wheeled her to the bedroom and got her into bed. She passed out. I didn't know what was happening. I called Rita and got voice mail. She returned the call shortly and asked to speak to Tonee. They had a brief incoherent conversation. Rita told me to get her to emergency. I knocked on Vern's door. He helped me get her up the ramp and into the car.

The staff at Castle Hospital emergency was very good. They hooked Tonee up with fluids, took all kinds of tests and asked her questions to check her competency. Tonee was off by six months and 3200 years on the date. Lincoln was the president. She was in Pennsylvania waiting for her Daddee to come. I told the Doctor she had a crushed foot and the hospital should have current xrays and mri's on her. Tonee cooperated with all the tests, but refused a spinal tap. The Chief Doctor of the hospital came down and diagnosed Tonee with severe dehydration and malnutrition. Her body was turning septic. She would have died without treatment. Tonee was admitted. The next morning, her fluids were regenerated and she had landed back on the planet Earth.

She stayed three days till her condition was

stable enough for her to go home. The Doctors urged her to stop drinking and take better care of herself. Tonee needed to drink more non alcoholic fluids and to have a much better diet. She was ten pounds lighter than two years before when she broke her hip. Tonee was scared, but not enough to totally cut off her wine. She said she would moderate. Tonee came home again, all bust up, in need of a new health regimen.

Tonee was a great healer. She was back on her feet walking within a month. She did some rehab and counseling on diet. This last episode was lengthy and so scary. I was exhausted and so worried that my Baby wasn't taking her falls so well anymore. Tonee worked hard with rehab to make sure she was walking properly and to regain muscle. She saw Linda occasionally, but felt isolated and lonely. With my work schedule, I helped the best I could. She cooperated with her Doctors to take supplements for her bones. As always, Tonee rebounded stronger than before. She had the will of a wild woman who would not be denied.

Tonee saw Rita less frequently. Her primary Doctor prescribed all her meds and gave her cortisone shots in her knees when they hurt.

The house in Massachusetts finally sold. Mama had insisted that Tonee be on the will for the property, an equal share with the other three children of her husband Eddie. It wasn't a huge amount as Tonee had hoped, but she had money in the bank and wouldn't worry for a while. My work had been going well, so we had a period of less stress over money. I still had credit card debt built up since we moved to Hawaii and there was still a balance on Tonee's dentures. Tonee would need work some day on her upper mouth. She had one front tooth that was loose and kept breaking. Tonee would crazy glue it back in place. Dr. Mark replaced it and experimented with different adhesives, but it was a regular issue.

My Brother, Ken, always wore cowboy boots and hats, a look very different for Oahu. Tonee offered to make a hat band for Ken. Tonee taught herself how to bead and made a couple of hat bands that came out beautifully, surprising everyone. Ken was delighted and praised her enough to put a couple of the girls into worker mode. Over the next several months, Tonee had produced a dozen or more. A couple were absolutely remarkable. I had watched her with her careful and precise effort. If she didn't like the result, she would take it apart and go at it again. Smart and beautiful. What a woman. What a heart. I was very proud of her and told her so.

Ken would take us out to dinner as thanks. It was good getting together once in a while.

Tonee had birds in California. She researched and decided she wanted a cockatiel. She found a breeder in another town who had a good reputation. We bought a cage and found the breeder's house. Tonee selected one young male from the huge selection. We set the cage up next to Tonee. She had a gentle way with the bird, but he barely cooperated with resting on Tonee's shoulder like her prior birds had. He grew bigger and his wings were full. I got him a bigger cage. He would fly around the apartment, crapping everywhere. Kona was pretty good with him, but couldn't resist chasing when he was in flight. Tonee wanted to clip his wings so he couldn't fly off. I argued against it. He became harder to get back in the cage, clamping down with his beak in a surprisingly painful way when I tried to put him back. Tonee started to wonder if the noise and the mess was worth it. One afternoon, Kona chased him in flight, pushing the door to the outside wide open. The bird flew off as I chased him. He landed a few feet away. Just as I was reaching to grab him, Kona lunged and scared him to flight. Tonee and I watched as he made several swoops of our home before disappearing over the trees forever.

Tonee had been exercising and walking Kona every day. She began to check on starting some exercise classes again. She was doing better with her diet, but the pretzels and canned whiz cheese were a staple. She was conscious of walking Kona and maintaining control. She rarely fell. I watched her every step at home when I was there. Tonee would get upset that I was babying her.

I started to worry when Tonee would get tired enough to sleep by 11pm, much earlier than her usual bedtime. I asked her several times if there was anything different in her meds that would affect her. She'd get angry and stubborn and tell me it was not my business. Sometimes, she would get off her chair to walk to the kitchen and wobble. I jumped to help her. I started to help her each night if she'd let me, but she usually would get angry and tell me to let her be. One night, near midnight when I had to go sleep, I asked her if she was ready for bed so I could help her. I supported her arm as she was woozy, helping her to the bathroom. I left her to pee. I heard her crash and groan.

Tonee was lying face down in the bathroom, blood dripping from her face. Her glasses lay smashed beside her.

"Are you okay Tonee?"

"No."

Tonee was exhausted. I helped her sit up next to the shower wall. Her left arm hurt. I cleaned the blood off her face where her glasses had smashed into her eyebrow. She had a one inch gash above her eye that would need stitches. I wanted to get her to Emergency right away. She was too tired and wanted to sleep. I told her she needed help, that the gash on her face would leave a scar if it wasn't done properly now. There was no obvious break in her arm, but I was sure from her reaction that it was not good. I patched her eye and helped her to bed. We would go to the hospital in the morning.

Tonee had a compound fracture on her upper arm and a slightly cracked pelvis. The arm probably could heal on its own, but with the complication of her pelvis, the doctor told us recovery so she could walk would be much quicker with surgery on her arm. Tonee didn't want to wait three months to walk. She opted for surgery. I never saw the xrays on her arm and went along with the advice of the specialists. I was absolutely exhausted and should have stayed at the hospital and asked more questions to the doctors instead of finishing my full day at work while Tonee went into surgery. I stopped in after work, but she was fully asleep. The following morning, I went in to see her. She was totally bummed out. Her broken arm was in a sling, but she had no use of her arm. A nerve had been affected and she had no function in her left hand. This occurred in ten percent of surgeries. This had not been mentioned to us before the operation. Most patients would recover function within six months. Tonee would need two to three weeks in rehab. She caught pneumonia in the hospital which delayed her transfer to rehab.

Tonee was distraught. I tried not to show my frustration. I was angry at her, which was so unusual for me. This was an avoidable accident. I kept asking her the last week or two if she had a different medication that was affecting her. At the hospital, she told the Doctor that her primary physician had put her on an anti anxiety pill that made her drowsy. The repetitive injuries were taking a toll on Tonee. I felt helpless and depressed and exhausted. All I could do was go to work and sell cars and take care of Kona. She went to the same rehab facility as when she broke her hip. It was undergoing major renovations and was a mess. Tonee was weak from her injuries and the pneumonia. She was totally bummed by her useless arm. She asked me not to visit her and when I came back she was angry and insisted I stay away. She did not tell me till she came home that she had contracted a very dangerous bacteria at the rehab facility. She didn't want me to get sick and didn't want me to see her when she was constantly using the bathroom. She made friends with her roommate during her three weeks in rehab hell.

I finally picked her up and drove her home. She could walk now, but her arm was not functioning. Tonee came home still fighting the remnants of the c diff bacteria. I put plastic everywhere she sat or lay down.

She was referred to a specialist for nerve damage. Initially, she hated him and let him know it. Then they got along. Very slowly, she began to get reaction in her upper arm. It would be months before her fingers began to tingle and work again. Six months after her fall, after constant therapy, Tonee was up and kicking ass again.

Personally, I was toast. I worked sixty hour

weeks, shopped, cleaned, helped Tonee and fed her bugger dog. I was frightened she would fall again. I felt as fragile as she had been. The first day Tonee could walk up the stairs and drive and use two hands was a great day. Tonee kept up her rehab and kept going forward. She would go to her doctor every few weeks for cortisone shots to her knee. Her lower body was like a war zone.

We celebrated New Years with the hope that the coming year would bring prosperity and health.

Somehow, I had worked through the damage of the last year with one of my best sales years. I was looking forward to the new year being even more prosperous at work. Almost immediately, there was another major change in management, the fourth in less than three years at Audi. The new Boss was young, promising to change everything. From the language he used, it sounded like he would change everybody. I had survived a lot in my fourteen years in the car business and I had survived eight years with Tonee. I figured things would be okay. I didn't know how emotionally and physically exhausted I was and how much it would affect my performance.

Tonee had been campaigning for a new car. She complained that Raven, her RSX, was hard to get into, had too many blind spots and she didn't trust the brakes. It was a good car, better than I had been driving. Tonee started researching as did I. We sold Mazda down the street at a sister company. I went in one day and drove the new Mazda 3. It was an impressive car. Tonee said all the research she did showed the new Mazda as an outstanding value. I went to my credit union and got a pre approval for a new car. Tonee was so excited the day I brought her down to test drive and look at colors and features. She absolutely loved the new Mazda. A couple of days later, she was driving her new pearl gray Mazda. She named her Lola. The car was nicely optioned, a real good car. Tonee was all smiles. She took pictures of Raven and placed an ad on Craig's List with the responses going to me. The payments were double what the Acura was. I would do almost anything to make Tonee happy and safe. My beautiful wife had her new car. Kona approved.

Tonee was getting around quite well. She couldn't wait to show her car to everyone, especially Linda who always drove an old beater even though she and Dan had a beautiful house near the sea. Tonee's energy was good. She had her left arm back. She started an exercise class. She advertised on Ebay a lot, selling off much of the jewelry she had been accumulating the last few years. She started looking for a job. She was concerned over finances, as was I.

I had been in the top three in sales at Audi the last two years. Last year was my best income wise, despite my mood over Tonee's health. January started off well and then fell in the shitter. My paychecks were still good, feeding from residual commissions from December. I had my first negative write up at Audi in two years, for poor sales. The new boss was going by the book to get things changed his way. He kept talking negatively about age and experience. He was the kind of guy you could like as he was smiling at you and sticking a knife in your gut and twisting. I had been through other lousy managers. I figured I could deal with this one.

My February paychecks were bad. I had to rely

on Tonee to make rent. To make matters worse, Vern called me to sit down one morning. He said his son was going to finally move here from Vegas and he would be taking our space. We had been very good tenants for seven and a half years. He said he would allow us to take our time to find the proper place to move to. When I told Tonee, she freaked. I told her it would be good in the long run and we could find a place on level ground so Tonee would be away from those dangerous eighteen steps to the street.

Two days later, Vern called me and told me we had one month to move. I told him that his timing was not good relating to our cash flow. He didn't care. What an asshole. I wasn't totally surprised, just completely shocked at his lack of compassion. He and I were not buddies, but he and Tonee had gotten along well. I didn't know how I'd tell Tonee. An hour later, Vern came down to make sure Tonee had gotten the message. Tonee freaked. I asked Vern to leave. An hour later, he came down with a check for five hundred dollars to help with our move.

Tonee was mad at me and worried about every detail of moving the amount of stuff we had accumulated. I told her Vern could not force us out in thirty days if we hadn't found our place. Tonee went into search mode for apartments in the Kailua area. We knew we would be spending more money. I told Tonee I would look at any property she was interested in. Tonee wrote a reference letter and had Vern sign it. I had never had a good move. I figured this would be no better. All I could do was go to work the long hours and produce like I always had.

We looked at a couple of places that Tonee didn't like. She found another a few blocks away that was totally on ground level with parking off street. She went and looked at it on her own and liked it a lot. I went with her for a second visit a couple of days later. It was close to a bar/restaurant and the main street. I was worried about noise. I hadn't even noticed the bus stop out front. She made an appointment for us to meet the landlord. She was a tough Korean business woman who was pretty straight forward if you could understand what she was saying. The rent was four hundred dollars more than we had been paying. We would make it work. Tonee interviewed some movers and found a church affiliated company. She liked and trusted the man and his price was fair. We set a date to move three days before the end of the month on my day off.

Tonee went into do it mode, shopping for curtains and new dinner ware. Our king size bed was too big and getting old and had taken more than a few dumps. I answered a credit card offer and had some money. I set up to have a queen size bed delivered and finally bought an HD tv and set up to have the cable and phone service wired before we moved.

I asked Tonee to wrap my Israeli artifacts. Ken and Lynette came over with a hoard of shipping boxes their neighbor had used. We offered Ken and Lynette our dining room table which they accepted. The movers were to pack half the house. She gave me the you left me to pack everything the last time look. She was angry and scared. I would hug her. We would tell each other things would be okay. My sales in March were better, but not good. We ate into savings and credit cards.

Tonee had packed four large boxes herself and marked them tag sale. They weighed a ton. I don't know how she handled them at all. She asked me to put them on the lanai. I moved them one after the other and wished I hadn't. Tonee kept filling plastic bags for rubbish and the Salvation Army. In my limited time off, I did what I could to organize for a structured move. We were going into a space with one and a half less rooms. I had a picture of how things would fit in the living room and bedroom. There was one extra bedroom for storage. Tonee was so nervous, but she channeled it into progress. The night before the move, she worked till eight and then we sat down and drank wine. There was a lot of "I love you" the last few weeks and some good hugs. We tried to stay upbeat. Tonee's anger would flare and usually go away. I had Tonee promise me she would be careful tomorrow and to let me and the movers do everything. I was so afraid she would hurt her arm again.

Tonee had a little soup for dinner. The wine helped her relax. We were ready for bed at midnight. Tonee cleaned up and was heading to the bedroom when she fell on the carpet.

"Are you Okay?"

"No. My hip hurts."

Tonee had fallen on her good hip. She was so tired she didn't want to go to the hospital yet. She asked me to cover her so she could rest. I brought her a pillow and a blanket and lay down on the carpet next to her.

"We're fucked. I can't believe it. We're so fucked." was all Tonee said.

A few hours later, the pain was extreme. I called an ambulance and Tonee went to Castle Emergency. She had a small fracture in her right hip. She told me to leave her and take care of the move.

The movers came at nine. It was an extreme hell day. The movers ended up packing more than they expected. The manager was compassionate that Tonee was hurt. He charged just two hundred dollars more. I gave him the $200 extra and our old bed and frame and tv. Vern was all over the place with the movers. He didn't give a shit that Tonee was hurt again. I tried not to antagonize him. I simply wanted him out of my life. He kept telling me how well he was treating us.

I put Tonee's plants and some fragile boxes in her RSX and was ready to drive over to the new place, but the transmission stuck. I remembered from sales training and asked Vern for a tiny screwdriver. I stuck it into a little spot near the shifter, getting it into gear. I drove to the new place and unpacked. I could not get the car into reverse so I left it in front of the new place. I walked the few blocks back and kept going. All we needed was a blown transmission. I felt like we were cursed.

At the end of the day, the old place was empty. The move was moderately orderly. Boxes had been marked and moved to the kitchen or spare bedroom or storage on the side of the house. Furniture fit in the way I expected. I thanked the guys for a great job. I made one last trip back to get Kona and the stuff from the refrigerator and freezer. Goodbye Herr Vern.

I visited Tonee at the hospital around eight o'clock. I went through emergency because regular visiting hours were over. Tonee was in bed, so heavily medicated, she could barely say "I love you Daddee." Surgery would be in the afternoon the next day. I kissed my wife goodnight and promised things would be okay.

I couldn't believe it. I felt so bad for Tonee. I went to the new home, kicked the dog and drank some wine. It was a good night to cry. My woman would not be lying next to me in our new home for another month. God, what a series of shit. She deserved so much better. My baby had the heart of a lion angel. Kona slept on the new bed with me. I was so tired, it pushed me past the fresh horror to a necessary sleep.

I visited Tonne's room before going to work in the morning. I kissed her gently on the lips. She was so medicated, she couldn't hold her head up. She was slinked sideways in her bed.

"The move was okay Tonee."

She barely responded before falling asleep. I went to the nurse in charge. She insisted they weren't over medicating Tonee. She was following the directions of the floor doctor. I asked to have the doctor call me. It felt bizarre being at work with Tonee in the hospital again. I told my immediate boss what was happening. He told me to do what I needed to do to take care of my family.

The Floor Doctor called me and said he would monitor Tonee's medication personally. When I saw Tonee again at seven o'clock, after surgery, she was just slightly conscious. I talked to the nurse and told her things were not right. She insisted they were not overdoing it. She said Tonee was asking for more pain medication when she was awake. I sat with Tonee holding her hand. The tv was on extra loud on food channel. I lowered the volume. The nurse came in and said they needed to change her diaper. I waited outside down the hall. Two of them came out of the room laughing at something. I went back in, but Tonee could not stay awake. Tonee would be transitioned to rehab in a day or two. After Tonee got C diff at the Honolulu rehab, I wanted to know what was available on the windward side. I asked to have someone call me the next day. I asked again to have the doctor call me about her medication.

A woman in charge of transition from the

hospital called. There was a facility in Kaneohe that was half nursing home and half rehab. They did not have as intense a program for rehab as the other facility in Honolulu. She told me Tonee should be ready to leave the following day.

I met the surgeon in the morning when I was visiting Tonee. She said the surgery went great and she spent extra time sealing the wound cleanly. She said Tonee should be able to put full weight on both legs immediately. I told her she was so over medicated she couldn't lift her head, never mind stand on her feet. The surgeon said she had no responsibility for in hospital treatment.

Tonee was slightly conscious that morning. She asked me where she was, what had happened. I told her she was in the hospital and just had surgery on her hip. I said Kona was okay and the new apartment was nice. The nurse came in. She said they had tried to get Tonee out of bed earlier, but she wouldn't cooperate. I tried not to swear, but I told that woman I was very displeased with the care. She shrugged her shoulders. She said Tonee kept talking about Daddy and was mumbling to someone from her childhood. I told her you had over drugged her. I stayed with Tonee till she fell back to sleep.

The next morning, I met with the woman in charge of the transition to rehab. She said, because the Kaneohe facility was not considered a full time rehab, that we would have to pay for transportation there and that the facility would charge $40 per day copay. I said that didn't make sense. I would not have Tonee go back to the Honolulu rehab where she got so sick. The transfer would be in the afternoon. I asked them to call me when it was done.

I received a call about 2:30 in the afternoon. The woman I spoke to earlier was frantic. She said

Tonee was acting irrationally and refusing to be moved. I told her to let me speak to Tonee. A young girl got on the phone frightened to death.

"Daddy. Come get me. They're trying to kill me."

"Tonee, do you know where you are?"

"I'm in jail. I got shot. They're trying to hurt me."

"Tonee, relax. No one will hurt you. I love you Baby. You're in the hospital. You broke your hip. They are going to bring you to a different place where I can visit you. Is that okay?"

"Okay Daddy."

"You'll get in the car?"

"Okeedokee."

I spoke to the woman and told her that Tonee needed to be handled carefully and to have Kaneohe call me when she arrives. I did not hear from anyone else till I showed up at the new place. Tonee shared a room with a woman who just had a stroke. Tonee was more conscious, but was still confused about the last couple of days. Dinner was brought in. Tonee and I shared a decent meat with gravy and potato plate. I didn't know it would be the only good dinner they'd serve.

I spoke to the head nurse and the nurse directly in charge of Tonee. I explained the problems we had at Castle with her being zombied with medication. They asked if that explained her odd behavior when she arrived. Tonee was tired and went to sleep. Outside her room, the elderly walked the halls and sat in wheelchairs staring, passing another day.

The next morning, Tonee was slouched in bed with drool down her mouth. The only word she spoke was "Daddy." I talked to the nurse and the head nurse and asked them what the hell was going on with her medication. I was sick of this treatment. They said they would have to speak to the Doctor who was not available. I asked to speak to someone from rehab. A young woman came over and said Tonee would get two sessions a day on the weekdays. I left for work feeling helpless.

In the evening, Tonee was semi conscious. She knew where she was and that she had hurt herself again. She asked about the move. She smiled when I told her Kona liked the place. The nurse said she barely ate and they went by a set schedule with her medication. They had some leeway if the patient was in too much pain. I asked Tonee how she felt. She said she would like a pain pill. I stayed for an hour. Tonee got another pill and dozed off.

The next morning, Tonee was in a zombie state again. I spoke to the nurse and I spoke to rehab. They said Tonee was not cooperating with rehab. I told her Tonee couldn't do anything if she was over drugged. I asked to have the Doctor in charge call me.

A woman who was in charge of patient welfare and transition in and out of the facility came. I told her about the over medication at Castle and here. The woman was concerned that if there was no progress in rehab, Medicare might not keep her there. A meeting was set at the end of the week to discuss Tonee's progress. I said I would certainly be there. I spoke to the head nurse again. She insisted they were not over drugging my wife.

The meeting was Friday at 10:30. I was early. Tonee was barely awake. She couldn't hold her head straight. The nurse helped Tonee get into a wheelchair. I pushed Tonee down the hall to a large room with a big long table. There were ten other people in attendance. None of them was the Doctor in charge.

Their concern was that Medicare would not allow her to stay unless she showed progress with rehab. I sat next to Tonee. Her eyes were barely open. She did not speak. Her head was slouched to the side. I told them how Tonee had been over drugged at Castle and this facility was continuing the same way. I asked them how Tonee could possibly do rehab for walking if she couldn't even stand up. They agreed I had a good point and they would look into it. I was told Tonee had a followup visit the following Tuesday with the surgeon. She would have to be transported both ways.

I felt like an idiot, helpless, in a system that could kill my wife.

The visit to the surgeon was a mess. I was at work, a big mistake. Tonee was brought there, semi conscious. I was told she was healing well. When I followed up with rehab a couple of days later, there was no progress. I found out that Tonee's status had been changed by the surgeon from full weight bearing to 25% for her right leg. She would not be allowed to walk. I asked what happened. No one knew. I called the surgeon's office. The surgeon was on the mainland for a week. I insisted I needed to know why Tonee's walking status had been downgraded other than the fact that she was over medicated. No one could give me an answer. I asked to have the surgeon contacted and have her call me directly. I did get a call from the surgeon the following day and she said she didn't remember the details, but she insisted Tonee never had been on full weight bearing status.

For a switch to a little good news, I walked

Kona down the street to a local auto repair shop. I was told they were honest. I spoke to the owner and told him my car was just down the street and I couldn't get it in reverse. He followed me over, got it into reverse and drove it back for a checkup. Ten minutes later, I received a call from the Craig's List ad for the Acura. A young woman wanted to come over later in the day to see the car. I told her a friend had borrowed it for a few days. I could call her when it was back. She said okay and I took her information. An hour later, Todd from the auto shop called and said the car was ready. It was a minor fix for $100, not the thousand plus I had expected. I called the girl and she said she would be down at five with her Father.

I washed the Acura with a hose. At 4:15, my customers arrived, drove the car and liked it. The Father asked if they could have a mechanic check it out. We drove it to the shop on the corner. They would inspect the car in the morning. Two days later, the check was in the bank. The loan was paid off with a few thousand left for us. Great timing. Lucky. Considering my paychecks lately, this would take a lot of pressure off.

When I visited Tonee in the evening, she was more awake. I told her we had to get her out of there asap, but that wouldn't happen if the drugs weren't minimized. Tonee went into grunt rehab mode. Tonee was supposed to be out in a week and a half. She had barely done anything more than stand up and sit down. I pushed for an appointment with the surgeon the day she returned, brought Tonee over myself, and had her status elevated back to 100% weight bearing. The surgeon denied ever putting Tonee on full walking before, even though the notes from Castle showed 100% when she was transferred to rehab. She had told me herself that Tonee could walk right after the surgery. What a lying sack of shit.

Over the next week, Tonee was alert and stable and attacked her rehab with purpose and desire. I brought Kona over one afternoon. I wheeled Tonee out to the garden and she and the puppy dog made nice. The sun was out. The flowers were beautiful. Tonee had twenty minutes of pleasure before returning to the nursing home for her last several days of rehab.

I picked Tonee up on Sunday morning as I was told to do. They had lost most of her nice clothes I had brought over. The nurse didn't know she was leaving. It took a couple of hours to get them in motion. I had Tonee hold her release papers as I wheeled her out the door to the passenger seat of her new car. This was a very good day. Tonee smiled wonderfully and said hello to Lola.

Kona went wild when he saw Mommy. I wheeled her from room to room. There were still boxes stacked in the kitchen and back storage room. I unpacked what I could. I did not want to unpack the kitchen area without Tonee's input.

"You did a good job Bobbie. I'm proud of you. I love you so much. Thank you."

I asked Tonee if she wanted to be out in the sun. I wheeled her around the yard. It was windy and she asked to go in soon. The rest of the day was quiet; tv, kisses, and the dog. I was so happy to have her home. I hadn't seen her smile this much in several months.

There was no carpeting in this apartment except the bedrooms. There would be no more falls. I had a professional install grab bars for the toilet and shower. Tonee said she would be good and only use her walker when someone was with her. We arranged to have rehab visits to the house twice a week through Castle Hospital. Tonee had her face in the computer with the tv on. She had her little notebook by her side. Tonee was back in operation. I just hoped she wouldn't push it too much when I was at work and she was alone.

"Don't worry Bobby. I'll be good. Promise. Now get me some wine."

It was early May. Tonee recovered with an absolute vengeance for life. She dismissed her walker the first week, but kept her cane for a couple of more weeks. She cruised around in Lola with pride and style. She had a problem with her computer. She could not get into her Ebay or Yahoo accounts. Her passwords were not written down anywhere. She went to the repair store. They were helpless, but did tell her how to contact ebay and yahoo directly. I set Tonee up with a new Yahoo account so she was halfway there. Ebay had issues worldwide. It took Tonee a few weeks to get back up to speed with them.

Tonee started posting things for sale again. She had been in touch with the owner of a marketing company since last year. They reconnected and Tonee agreed to go to her Haleiwa home/office to get training on their computer and sales systems. Tonee couldn't do outdoor sales, but would be paid for part time phone sales out of our house. She would get hourly plus bonuses for performance. Tonee's worker girl was an interesting and beautiful woman. I went to Radio Shack and bought her a nice phone system with a headset. She absolutely loved it.

"Thank you Bobbie."

Tonee started calling from home. Her paid

hours were 9-2, but she generally put in a couple more hours than that. She was having difficulty with the company's software system. Her boss offered to come to Kailua for more training.

I had asked Tonee to work with me to clear the boxes from the kitchen. She was too busy, so I attacked them on my own, putting things away the best I could. Tonee would occasionally butt in and straighten out my thinking. The extra boxes were stored in the back room and the side of the house. Tonee did some rearranging of furniture and bought some plants to hang outside.

Tonee would get up at 8am and would be on the phone by nine. I was not allowed to watch tv while she was working. I enjoyed listening to her deep throated voice and laugh as she chased clients on the phone for appointments that her boss and other salespeople would go to. She was charming and relentless, getting cell numbers and emails and following people till they gave in or said no for the third time. She was professional and non stop once she kicked into action. The Tonee I witnessed must have been the girl who put herself through College and Grad School. She would be on the phone with her boss several times a day. Soon, appointments were being made at a solid rate. I was impressed. Tonee was sent a new Ipad as an extra reward for her efforts. Her first paycheck put a good smile on her face. What a great woman.

My work was failing. I had been written up three times for poor sales. June 2, I was called into the office and fired. I was shocked but not surprised. I asked to speak to the big boss. He said I should thank him for getting me out of there. He said I could apply for a position at the Jaguar store when it opened in July. My sales were miserable, far worse than I had ever done over five months. I reminded him that I was top sales last year and second the year before. He said I could pick my check up in the morning.

I couldn't imagine giving the news to Tonee. All I wanted was to take care of her. Overall, I had done okay, but Hawaii was an expensive place. My contributions to our family had been substantial, but that meant little in the present moment. We had almost no money in the bank, a more expensive apartment and a larger car loan. My sweat stank nervous. I didn't want to go back to Infiniti or Acura. I didn't think I would do better there. I cleared my desk, said goodbye to a few people and drove home to face the Tonee.

Tonee was still on the phone working when I arrived. She gave me the why are you here look. I told her I was fired. She was not too surprised. She hugged and kissed me and said we'd be okay.

I phoned a friend of mine at the Volvo Dealership. He said there were only four or five sales people and they were opening a second store in Kaneohe soon. That was very different from Audi which had doubled the sales staff since January with no increase in sales. My friend gave me the name of the manager, Jim. I tried to reach him by phone, but only found voice mail. The next morning, I shaved extra well, drove down to Ala Moana, and waited till Jim could see me. We talked for a half hour. He said I could start today if I wanted. I told him I would start Friday. The only thing I asked for was to make sure the health insurance was in place July 1. Jim said he would make it happen.

I picked up a rye bread and some bagels at the nearby bakery. I hoped things would go well at Volvo. The last few months there had been very upbeat. The ownership was new and willing to invest strongly. This would be very different from where I had been.

Tonee was surprised and delighted at my success. There was some fear in her voice and face. I just wanted to hug her and make love and give her a comfortable life.

"I love you Tonee. We're going to be okay."

Tonee put her headset back in place and attacked her client list. Her followup was absolutely consistent.

I started at Volvo Friday morning. Everyone seemed nice. I sold my first car on my third day. The deal fell through and I was still fighting to earn my first dollar. I kept asking about the health insurance and Jim said he would look into it. The business office was completely new and didn't know what they were doing. The place was chaos on a daily basis. One of the salesmen had an argument with Jim and quit. He had told me the day before that he was ready for a change. At least I had my own desk now.

Tonee brought some milkweed plants home one day and placed them on the kitchen table. She showed me the six caterpillars that were munching on the leaves.

"In two weeks, they'll make little cocoons. Ten days after that, they will be Monarch Butterflies. Isn't that cool Bobbie?"

I loved her mind and energy. She was moving around like she'd never been hurt. My woman made me happy in my misery.

"I made my first sale today Bobbie."
"I'm so proud of you Tonee."

My first month at Volvo was okay, better than I'd done at Audi. My second month was a dud. Tonee got mad a few times and went into a rage when it came time to write a rent check. She could be very demeaning, but I knew it was one of the angry girls, her defense mechanism. Mostly, Tonee was solid and upbeat, kicking it on the phone at work.

Her first couple of butterflies fell from their cocoons when they opened. Their wings were stuck in their own goo. They hung around for a while but could not fly. Tonee bought some light netting and experimented with it so the butterflies would have something to latch onto as their cocoons disintegrated. The next couple of butterflies were perfect and beautiful. Tonee would hold them by their wings and let them free after the first day. She put some milkweed plants outside hoping the Monarchs would return home to lay their eggs.

Tonee bought more plants and caterpillars. Linda came over a couple of times to see Tonee's new babies. Tonee was happy. I enjoyed watching the process. The first time I saw a cocoon forming was like magic before my eyes.

Tonee started to complain about a stiffness in her left shoulder. Dr. Lerner was on vacation for a couple of weeks. When he returned, he gave her a cortisone shot in the shoulder. It was August. Tonee's job would be over at the end of the month. She worked extra hard to maximize her sales and commissions.

Finally, I got lucky and hot at work. I had a two
week period where I sold a car every day. Tonee was
delighted. She asked if she could get her hair done.
"Of course Baby."

Tonee's shoulder continued to bother her. She
was in a lot of pain. Dr. Lerner said he would have her
get an MRI. It took two weeks for the insurance
company to say no. It was too expensive. It took
another week to set an appointment for the cat scan.
This was taking too long.

Tonee finished with her job and kind of sat
back with a look of satisfaction. Her shoulder was
hurting so much she had trouble getting in and out of
bed. She wouldn't let me help her. She said it hurt too
much.

One morning, I was up early. I knew a couple
of the cocoons were ready and I wanted to see one
emerge. One of the butterflies was already out and
still in a fetal position stuck in its own juice on the
floor.

I woke Tonee to help. She was angry that I
woke her. I told her a butterfly needed help. She gave
me a pissed off look. It took her a few minutes of
writhing on the bed to get to her feet. She went to the
couch and sat down where the little baby lay in a
butterfly ball on the floor. She picked the little baby up
in her hand and felt it. Then she blew her gentle
breath on the little baby until the wings began to
unfold perfectly. The little butterfly clung to Tonee's
finger. Tonee stood and placed him on the screen of
the window where she flapped in young glory. What
an amazing thing. Tonee looked up from her seat on

the couch and thanked me for waking her to help. She went back to bed to sleep. I went to work.

Tonee wasn't able to drive because she couldn't move her neck properly. I helped her into Lola and drove to Castle for the cat scan. I told her she'd probably need a good chiropractor. The cat scan took an hour. We were watching tv at dinner time when Dr. Lerner called. Tonee got a look on her face.

"Are you sure doctor?"

Tonee hung up the phone.

"It's Cancer."

I hugged my Baby and told her she'd be okay. We would get through it. She had an appointment the following afternoon with Dr. Lerner. I had a friend who's sister had cancer of the bone. It was not good. I tried to be positive and hopeful. Tonee was scared, but did not cry. She kind of looked into the distance.

The first look I had of Dr. Lerner when he saw Tonee in the office gave me a sick heart. Tonee went in first and said I could come in a few minutes. Tonee went into the office alone. I saw Dr. Lerner's face and he looked at one of his assistants like he dreaded the coming conversation. He hunched up his shoulders and walked into the office to meet Tonee.

Tonee had cancer in her neck and spine. They would need more tests to find where it originated and how far it had spread. Dr. Lerner suggested three Oncologists. We agreed on the choice. Dr. Lerner said he had a decent sense of humor for someone in that field. He had offices in Honolulu and Kailua. His office would call with an appointment. He gave Tonee prescriptions for pain. Dr. Lerner said he would start to set up the appointments for further testing.

I spoke to Dr. Lerner outside the room. He said

whatever it was it was not good.

I told Jim at work the next morning that my wife had cancer. It came out in a cry. Jim's mother had been slowly dying of cancer in Texas. He was afraid to visit her. He told me whatever I needed to do, he would back me. I said there would be times I'd need to be out of work. I also told him I needed a stable paycheck.

Tonee had an appointment at Queen's Hospital with Dr. Cho, the Oncologist, late Friday morning. The nurse asked us to be early to fill out paperwork. We got a little lost and arrived just on time. Tonee was walking with a cane. It was a long distance down the halls. Tonee was deliberate and complete filling out the sheets of questions. We ran into a friend of mine from Audi. I never knew she had cancer. She said she had been in remission for two years. All around us, the large room was filled with very sick people. I saw one beautiful woman in tears when she received the new results of her blood work. I so hoped we would not be in that light. I held Tonee's hand. The doctor was running an hour late. He was very deliberate and complete with his patients.

Tonee went in first so she could get a feel for Dr. Cho. After ten minutes, I went in. The doctor explained that they would need more testing to know exactly what was happening to Tonee and how to attack it. Tonee said she was in terrible pain. The doctor wanted to admit her to Queens Hospital immediately to control the pain and fast track the tests. Tonee told him Dr. Lerner had started to set up some testing at Castle. Tonee said she wanted at least one day at home to get ready for the hospital. Dr. Cho had his nurse call Dr. Lerner's office and

Castle and find out what was happening with the tests. By the time we left, we knew Tonee would be at Castle Tuesday and Wednesday for testing and see Dr Cho at his Castle office Wednesday afternoon. His demeanor was friendly and direct. He went from room to room all day with news good and bad for his very sick patients.

I asked Tonee if she had called Linda and if she wanted to call Ken and Lynette. She wanted her privacy till she knew what was happening. All I wanted to do was hug her and protect her and be with her forever.

"I love you Tonee."

"I love you Robert."

I lay in bed watching her sleep wondering how many days I had with her next to me.

It made me sick being at work away from my woman. I was unfocused and incapable of doing my job well. I tried because we needed the money.

Tonee had her glass of chilled white wine while watching tv. She was having trouble with the computer. I offered to help. She said the coordination with her fingers and her eyes was off. I told her she'd get better. Tonee said the pain pills she had weren't good enough. Kona lay at her side. When he put his head on her lap, she pet him as if it were an effort.

I prayed for our time together. She was such a beautiful soul. I had been so blessed to be with her. I tried not to cry in front of her.

Tonee did her tests on Tuesday. She said they tortured her with the positions she had to lay in.

"It hurt so much Bobbie."

Wednesday, she had another MRI early in the morning. Linda had taken her in so I could go to work.

I came home at noon for the two o'clock appointment. Tonee said it was cancelled. I asked her who called and why was it cancelled. She said she wasn't sure. I called Castle and spoke to a nurse at Dr. Cho's office. She said the appointment had not been cancelled. Tonee dressed and did her makeup. The office in Kailua was more crowded than the one at Queen's. They were two hours behind schedule. Tonee started to get tired and cold. She was in a lot of pain. The nurse brought her a wheelchair and a big blanket. We finally went in to a room to wait another forty five minutes for Dr. Cho.

Dr. Cho stuck his face in and said hello. He would be back in a minute. Finally, he came in and studied his computer screen. He said the cancer had spread over the bones in her upper body and up and down her spine. There were also a couple of traces in her liver. They could not determine where the cancer originated, which made it difficult to know how to best attack it. He said it most probably was cancer, but they couldn't officially pronounce it without a biopsy. He would set up a biopsy of the liver as soon as possible.

Tonee looked frail and tired in her wheelchair. I asked the doctor what the prognosis was. He said the outcome would most certainly be fatal.

I felt like I had been shot. Then I heard the beautiful voice of a young angel.

"Bobbie, I thought Dr. Cho was supposed to be a funny man. I didn't hear him say anything funny. Did you?"

The doctor asked if there were more questions. I asked if he had any idea of her life span. The doctor said the biopsy might help determine that. He wrote several prescriptions and said we could pick them up at the front desk.

I kissed Tonee. Her eyes were scared. She held her jaw tightly. She was a little white. I wheeled her down the hall and past the front desk and into the hall outside the office. I went back in and got the prescriptions. I felt like I was in an out of body experience. Tonee was mad at me for leaving her outside. I told her if I got that kind of news, I would want privacy. She told me not to do that again.

I cried in the car as I drove us home. Tonee asked me not to cry, to be strong for her. It would help her be stronger. What a woman.

I left her at the apartment and told her I would get the meds. She said I could get them another time. I knew she had stronger pain medication coming and I needed to go out and cry my heart out.

The doctor and nurse had not filled in the full home address, so the pharmacy could not dispense without Tonee's id. I rushed home and returned before they closed. Why was this happening to my beautiful woman? Why had she been put through the life she had?

Tonee thanked me for my efforts. I looked in her beautiful blue eyes. How much longer?

Tonee finally went to bed. She looked so young and wonderful lying next to me. I wondered how many more nights could she be with me?

She was having trouble being comfortable. In the middle of the night, she rose to sit in her chair with the tv.

"I might be in less pain out there."

The next day at work, I told Jim my wife was dying. I did not know how long it would be. Why was I at work? I left early to shop for food and wine and to be home with my beautiful woman. Kona was not sure how to be with his Mother. He was used to her smothering him with attention. I went to the bedroom and called Ken and Lynette and told them the news. It came out in a cry. I could not talk further.

Tonee said it might be good if she stayed in the hospital for a little while so they could get her pain under control. I had bad memories of Castle where they made her a zombie with the meds. I was terrified that if she left, I would never sleep next to her again. I don't remember what I said to her, but she stayed home a few more days. One night, Tonee said something about Linda bringing her to Castle the next day. I passed it off as fantasy.

The next morning I showered for work. Tonee got up and asked if I could help her take a shower. The chair was in the shower for her to sit on and slide into. I helped her undress and get into the shower. She used her baby wash and shampoo. I toweled her dry and helped her walk to the bedroom where she started to dress. I saw the large bruise on her right side where she fell rising from the toilet the night before. She had a little overnight bag. I asked her where she was going. She said Linda was taking her to Castle. She seemed like a little girl excited for the change. I called Linda. She apologized for going behind my back. I said I just wanted the best care for Tonee. I was terrified this would be her last time at home. I asked Linda if she had some thongs or slippers Tonee could use. Her feet were so swollen, she couldn't wear anything she had.

Linda arrived. I kissed Tonee goodbye and left for work. I was absolutely useless. All I wanted was to be with my wife.

The Floor Doctor called me from Castle in the afternoon. He said Tonee had been dehydrated and malnourished and that the damage in her neck had deteriorated badly from the last x rays. There was the possibility the spine could snap and she would require a ventilator if it was authorized. He asked if there was a consent order. I told him Tonee would never want to be left on a machine. The Doctor told me the biopsy results were in. It was Cancer, but they still did not know what type or where it had originated. I told the doctor that Tonee had no appetite the last month. He said he would prescribe marinol, a thc based pill that sometimes helped the appetite. I also told the Doctor that her last time at Castle, they had messed her up with meds. He said he would be very careful. I thanked the doctor for his call. I walked outside to cry and walked around the block a couple of times. When I returned to work, I asked if I could leave early.

When I reached Castle hospital, I promised myself I would not cry. I walked into Tonee's room. Her dinner tray was in front of her. She had her face full of noodle soup, liquid and noodles dripping down her chin. I couldn't stop laughing. Then she ate the fruit and she and I split the chocolate cake.

"How do you feel Baby?"

"It was good to eat."

Tonee left all her jewelry home except for her wedding ring.

The Doctor had already left for the day. I spoke to her nurse who said Tonee was a perfect patient. I stayed in her room for a while till she got real woozy. She had trouble finding a comfortable position for her neck. I helped her put towels on either side to keep her stable. I kissed her goodnight.

"I love you Tonee."

"I love you Bobbie."

I met the Doctor the next morning. I said when Tonee was home, I didn't know how to help her in and out of bed without hurting her. He said he would have the rehab people meet with us.

Later in the day, a woman from the palliative care called me and asked if there was anything she could do to help. I told her no. The next morning, two women from rehab tried to show me how to get Tonee in and out of bed. After a couple of tries, it was obvious that Tonee didn't have the strength anymore to walk. Every day, she seemed to go away a little more. It was absolutely terrifying.

I never saw Tonee cry through this horror. She looked so beautiful. Linda came in to visit. Tonee's eyes lit up. Linda noticed Tonee's swollen fingers. Her skin was puffed up on either side of her wedding ring. Linda asked if it was okay if she tried to take it off. Tonee shook her head yes.

The ring wouldn't come off at first. I gave Linda a little vaseline that we used for her chapped lips. The ring finally came off. Linda handed it to me.

I called the woman from palliative care. I had questions on Tonee's options for Hospice care. We set an appointment to meet early the next morning in Tonee's room. When I arrived, the nurse and the doctor and the palliative woman and her boss were all gathered. This was a meeting to discuss Tonee's near future.

The senior palliative person stood beside Tonee and spoke outlining the damage in Tonee's neck area. She said Dr. Cho was recommending she go to Queen's for x ray therapy to relieve pressure on the nerve in Tonee's neck which was probably causing the most pain. She said Tonee was in a fatal situation and could die in a day or at most six months.

She could be moved to a hospice facility, but there would be nothing further done to make her better, only pain management. If she did hospice at home, there would be very limited help that would be available for her daily care. I would have to be the care giver or pay for a service. I didn't think Linda or Ken and Lynette would volunteer for much help. I had no idea how to care for the bedridden. She asked if there was a consent order. I told her Tonee did not want any machines keeping her alive. She looked at Tonee and asked and Tonee nodded her head in agreement. She looked like a tiny girl in that bed surrounded by all these people. I said I thought the move to Queens made the most sense. Tonee shook her head okay.

I received a call at work saying Tonee would be transferred to Queens at 5:30pm. I said I would be at Castle before she left. At four, I was just leaving work and they said Tonee was being transferred now. I asked to speak to Tonee. I told her she was going to the other hospital now. Did she want me to meet her there? Tonee said yes please. I drove home to take care of Kona, then drove back to town to be with my love.

Queens hospital was huge. It took a while to find the right room. Tonee was settling in. The nurse was taking vitals. They were doing their thing to make Tonee a part of the system. I asked for a turkey sandwich. Tonee wasn't hungry, but I was. Dr. Cho called the room and spoke to me. He said Dr Lee would be in charge of her x ray therapy. Someone would call me in the morning. Tonee was a little flustered by the move. She had a private room in the Oncology ward. These people seemed very proficient.

"I love you Tonee."

"I love you Robert."

I stayed an hour, then kissed her goodnight. I asked the nurse to be especially careful with her neck. It was a long crying walk to the car.

Kona was excited to see me. He went outside and did his thing. I gave him a carrot. It was time to shower and drink some wine and watch tv and cry.

Tonee's new hospital was okay. They had room service for food. The nurse said they could move a cot inside Tonee's room if I wanted to stay over. Tonee was strong and loving. Through this entire run to death, she was careful and polite with everyone, including her nurses. The only time she got angry was when the rent check was due. It was like an auto reaction that went away almost immediately.

"Bobbie, I'm scared."

All I could do was tell her I loved her and be with her. She was still registering 8-10 on her pain meter. I asked Tonee if she wanted to talk to a Rabbi. She said yes. I called the Synagogue where we were married. The new Rabbi said he would be over in the afternoon. Again, I went to work, leaving my beautiful woman behind.

I called the synagogue the next day. The Rabbi said he had gone to see Tonee, but she was asleep. He sat with her and prayed. He went back again in the evening and she was still asleep. I told him it was okay to wake her, that she wanted to talk to him. He returned again and had a peaceful talk with Tonee. I thanked him very much.

I was asked if I could be at the hospital the next day from 10-12 to help transition Tonee into her x ray therapy.

The nurse gave Tonee an extra pain pill because the session downstairs was long and she might be put in some uncomfortable positions. Tonee looked scared as her gurney was wheeled down hall after hall and two elevators to the downstairs x ray department. We were put in a cold room. A nurse took information and said Dr Lee would be in shortly. She said the session would take about an hour once they started.

I held Tonee's hand. I knew she didn't want to be there. Dr. Lee came in and talked to us. She explained that they had to make a facial mask for Tonee to be able to hold her in a precise position for the radiation. The mask would take a half hour with her head facing up, completely stationary. Then they would be another twenty minutes mapping the site for radiation. She asked Tonee if she was ready and Tonee said no, not today. Dr Lee was disappointed, but took it in stride. She said she'd be back in a few minutes.

I kissed Tonee. She looked up at me.

"Bobbie, it's time."

I didn't know what she meant. Was it time for her to die?

"It's time for me to go home."

I almost lost it completely. I so wanted her home. But for how long?

Dr Lee returned. She asked me if I had seen any of the images. I hadn't. On her little computer, she brought up image after image. I could see the upper neck where the bone structure looked like it was chewed on. The dark spots were cancer. One shot showed her entire spine with black up and down right into her tail bone. She showed where the cancer was causing pressure on the nerve in her neck. The therapy was to attack that area to relieve the pressure and some of the pain. She said bone cancer was always terminal; their job was to make quality of life better. I told Dr Lee that Tonee and I would talk and let her know if she would continue. Dr Lee said she would reserve time tomorrow for that possibility.

I wanted Tonee to try. We talked for a little while upstairs. She surprised me by agreeing to try again tomorrow. I called and let Dr. Lee know. I made appointments to speak to a couple of representatives from local Hospices. One was recommended by Queens, the other strongly recommended by Dr Lerner.

The first appointment for the Queens Hospice was at the hospital with Tonee present. The woman was a Haole who had moved here from the mainland in the last six months. She said Tonee could stay at their facility in Honolulu or at home. She emphasized that they were very liberal in their pain control approach. The whole purpose was the end of life on her terms. She was pretty aggressive for the islands, dissing on the nursing staff for keeping Tonee in the level of pain she was in. She also said they were non profit as opposed to some of the others who claimed to be, but were not. I asked Tonee if she had any other questions. I thanked the woman for her time. I would let her know when we were ready to make a decision.

I met with Island's Hospice at our apartment the next morning. The services were similar. He said they had volunteer service, but he couldn't guarantee I would get enough help. They were non profit. They had four facilities available or Tonee could stay at home. Their pain control policy was also liberal. He was soft spoken, almost the way I sold cars. I told him I would let him know. They did have one facility in Kailua, but it was small and booked in advance mostly for family stays to take pressure off care givers.

I was early to the hospital to make sure Tonee

had enough medication and to calm her for the ordeal. She was so beautiful and accommodating. Her jaw clenched as the gurney went over bumps on the way down. Dr Lee and her staff wheeled Tonee into a small room with a big machine. Volunteers came over to carefully transition her to the platform of the machine.

Tonee needed to lie on her back with her neck position dead center, staring straight up. A mesh mask was put over her face and they formed a cast surface on top. Tonee would have to remain in place for twenty five minutes as the mask hardened. I held her hand.

"It hurts Bobbie."

"It's okay Tonee. It'll be done soon."

To Dr Lee's and my surprise, Tonee lasted the time. The mask would be ready for tomorrow at 7am. Tonee looked exhausted when she finally reached her room. I told her how proud I was of her. I would be there tomorrow morning before they brought her down. The plan was for four sessions of x ray.

"Bobbie, I don't know if I can do It."

"We'll give it a try."

I woke at five and left the house by 5:45am. Traffic was heavy. I didn't reach the hospital till just before seven. I rushed up to Tonee's room, but she was already gone. It took me fifteen minutes getting lost to reach my Baby in the basement. She was uncomfortable and looked exhausted and old. The technician had arrived early to start warming up the machine at 6am. Tonee was still waiting at 7:30. I gave her some water. I found a nurse and asked if someone could change her diaper. Tonee didn't get into the x ray room till eight. She was uncomfortable and looked exhausted and old. Again the volunteers switched her position onto the machine. They needed to move Tonee up and sideways. The new mask was put over her face. She was trembling, clutching my hand. There were six bolts to hold the mask in place.

"Bobbie, are you there?"

"Yes baby. It'll be done soon."

Tonee lasted five minutes.

"Let me out. Daddee, I can't do this."

Dr Lee was a little upset because she had brought her team in extra early for the effort. Then she got over it and said they could try again tomorrow morning. I thanked her. We waited till someone came to bring us back upstairs. My work schedule was 1-8. It was nine am when we made Tonee's room. I asked the nurse for a cot. I ordered eggs and sausage and bacon and orange juice. The only thing that tasted real was the juice. Nasty food. Tonee had barely eaten in the last month or more. I had asked Queens to try the marinol. Nothing built her appetite.

"Don't be mad at me Bobbie."

"Why would I be mad at you? You're a lion. I'm so proud of you. It's your decision Tonee if you want to try again tomorrow."

"Okay Daddee."

Tonee lay asleep. The nurses would come every thirty minutes or so. They shifted her bed position every two hours to prevent bed sores. My cot was perpendicular to Tonee's bed so I could see her as I lay down to rest.

As I looked at my beautiful wife; for the first time, I could see the palour of grey-green in her face. She looked like a woman dying. It killed me.

I went into the hall and called Dr Lerner. Fortunately, he was readily available. I asked him how strongly he felt about Island Hospice. He said his experiences were good and that the physician in charge was a good man. He said he couldn't be specific, but he'd had experience with other hospices that were horrific.

I called John from Island Hospice and asked him to see if there was a room available now for Tonee in Kailua. He said he would call me back. I called down to Dr Lee and told her Tonee would not continue with the therapy. I told her I thought Tonee looked as if she were dying. Dr Lee did not disagree.

I went back to Tonee's room and cat napped for a couple of hours before going to work. When Tonee woke up, I told her there would be no more therapy downstairs.

"Oh, thank God."

"I'll be back in the morning Baby."

"Bobbie, I'm really scared."

"Me too, sweetheart. Do you want me to stay?"

"No. Go to work. You look so handsome."

The facility in Kailua was full. The choices were two facilities that would have four people per room or the nursing home she'd stayed in in Kancohe which would have two people per room. I hated that place. I hated to think of Tonee passing away in such an impersonal, noisy environment. The last possibility was hospice at home. It would be me doing her care with a little help a few times a week from the hospice staff. I would have to miss work. It frightened me thinking of having to do all the personal care for Tonee. I was so scared I wouldn't do it well and could hurt her more.

I asked John to see if Tonee could be placed in Kaneohe, the littlest evil. He would call me back.

I left work early to meet John at our house to sign papers for Tonee's transition into Island Hospice. He said they would accept her in Kaneohe. Tonee would transfer the next day once all the paperwork and a room were in order. I drove back to Queens to let Tonee know she would be moving again. When I told her she would be going back to Kaneohe, she said okay Bobbie. I couldn't picture my Baby dying in that institution. It was busting me up.

I stayed with Tonee for a while. I felt like I was counting our moments.

"I love you Daddeee."

"You're my special girl."

I was flustered and scared and grieving. It was late when I returned home. I fed Kona and took him for a walk around the neighborhood, causing every dog to bark. I was exhausted, but could not sleep well. I took another shower in the middle of the night, then watched a little tv. I wanted my beautiful woman home, alive and well, but it could never be. I could not imagine Tonee at that nursing home.

At seven in the morning, I called John from Island Hospice, and told him I wanted to do home hospice. John said he would make it happen. Tonee would be back home by late afternoon. Someone would have to be home to accept the equipment being sent over. I asked him to have them call to coordinate the deliveries.

I went to work. As soon as Jim came in for the Friday sales meeting, I told him my wife was coming home to die. I would probably be out of work for a couple of weeks.

I drove home, happier with a decision that my woman would be where she belonged. I cleared space and the kitchen table so Tonee could stay in the living room. The bed would be arriving by noon. Tonee would leave the hospital by 1:30, arriving by 2:30. The bed was late, showing up at one. The man assembled it quickly. The oxygen came in a different truck. A special mattress pad and portable table tray came next. I put sheets on the bed and a second sheet on top to help reposition Tonee. Kona was barking at everyone. I put him out back for a time out.

At 3:30, the ambulance brought Tonee home, smiling like a conqueror, her eyes adoring the sight of home. She grimaced on bumps as she was wheeled into the house. Kona went into a hyper bark. I put him out back. The nurse from the hospice arrived just in time to settle Tonee in. I signed a hundred papers. The ambulance left. The nurse was wonderful, explaining how to operate the bed and the oxygen. The packet of meds was delivered and she went into detail on each one, more types of pills than I'd seen before. As discussed, Tonee would have some liquid morphine and hydro morphone pills for pain. Other pills were for anxiety and fluid buildup and nausea and constipation and a bunch more.

I just wanted to hug Tonee and let her be alone with me and Kona.

The nurse said Tonee would have to be repositioned every couple of hours to prevent bed sores. She showed me how to do it. It seemed to put Tonee in an awkward position. She said another nurse would come over later who would be in charge of Tonee's case. She would show me how to clean and change Tonee's diaper. The under mattress vibrated, helping to prevent bed sores. The oxygen machine hissed as it worked. She showed me how to keep the breathing tube in place. Later, more supplies would be delivered for care and cleaning. I would have to supply clean linens and towels. As life was working lately, the washing machine out back had broken. My landlady promised to get it fixed asap.

The nurse left and Tonee and Kona and I were

alone at home together for a little while.

The other nurse came over and gave me more contact information. She showed me how to bathe and change Tonee. For the first time since I had helped Tonee out of the shower, two weeks back, I saw her naked body, bloated from all the iv's. Her whole right side back was black and blue, an extension of the bruise she took falling the night before she went to Castle. She had some tender spots on her back and bottom that could get worse if she were not adjusted properly on a regular basis. The nurse asked Tonee how her pain was.

"Ten"

The nurse, Joanne, gave her two pills and some liquid morphine. She said the morphine was fast acting but only lasted an hour. Before she left, Tonee's pain was much more tolerable. She said she would be back sometime the next day. She would come three times the first week and two times a week thereafter. She gave me the name and number of a local company who could provide hourly care at a rate better than most.

Over the next several days, she said I would receive visits from their chaplain and a counselor. I felt dizzy and overwhelmed, but the pleasure of having Tonee with me again was an overwhelming joy.

"I love you Tonee."

"I love you Daddeee."

I asked Tonee if she wanted the tv on and she said yes. I let Linda and Ken and Lynette know Tonee was back. They said they would visit soon.

I sat down and held her hand. I gave her sips of water and apple juice by straw. She didn't want any fruit or other food. Kona tried to get on her bed a couple of times. The first time, he hurt her by stepping on her. The second time, I helped him slide in next to Tonee. She rested her hand on him for a little while before Kona jumped off. Tonee had a tiny snore as she slept. I lay back in my recliner to close my eyes.

I called the woman from the temp service. She was very local. She would charge $15 per hour if her person stayed all day or $20 per hour for a short stint. I told her I would call her the next day once I understood the schedule better.

This whole horror was four weeks from the day Dr Cho gave us the death prognosis. Tonee had been in constant, extreme pain the whole time. The transitions from home to hospital to hospital to home was a terrible blur. All through this time, Tonee never cried that I saw. She was kind and appreciative and loving. Tonee always believed in an afterlife. This life had given her the toughest test from when she was a child. She was beautiful and classy.

I lit Shabbos candles, praying for Tonee to pass quickly out of her pain and to find her peace.

I slept in my bed in the other room for a few hours the first night. Then I used Tonee's recliner which I turned around so I could see her and hold her hand. It went further back than my recliner, so I was able to sleep a little. Tonee would dream and talk in her sleep. I could not understand many of her words, but the voices were mostly tiny and very young. A few times, she even giggled a little. Her face was smooth and simple as her six year old. When she opened her eyes for a peek, I would tell her I love you.

"Daddee."

Joanne came over in the late morning with an assistant. They bathed Tonee and changed her. She scolded me for leaving Tonee wet and not adjusting her position in bed. I got a fresh set of sheets. Tonee was leaking a little clear fluid on her right arm. Joanne said the towels had to be cleaned regularly. The fluids would develop a bad odor after a couple of days. I put a towel and one of the their barrier cloths under her arm. Joanne said she would be back in two days.

Linda came over in the afternoon for a few minutes. Tonee smiled and said Hey Girl. Linda asked if there was anything she could do. I asked if she could wash some sheets. Kona always barked when Linda came over. I put him outside for a little while.

A man came later in the day to fix the washing machine, but left saying he would have to order parts from the mainland.

Tonee mostly slept. Ken and Lynette came over in the evening. They had visited her at the two hospitals. Tonee lit up with the company but soon her head dropped to sleep.

The Rabbi came over a couple of times. The Hospice Chaplain also visited and prayed. She was remarkably upbeat.

I had the temp agency have the woman come over for an hour in the morning and evening. One night, Tonee was anxious and building up fluids in her mouth. I called the hospice and they told me which pill to give her. It helped. Each day, Tonee went a little further away. I was always by her side, holding her hand. Linda came over the third day Tonee was home and gave me a breather to leave the house. I drove to the beach and let the ocean water and sunlight ease my pain for twenty minutes.

The third night, Tonee's breathing was more animated. She was calling out for hours, sometimes screaming deep into the night.

"Daddeee. Daddeee."

"I'm here baby."

"Daddeee. Deddeee. I'm scared deddeee."

Her arms and legs were in motion. Sometimes, her eyes opened, but she did not see. She was so young.

"Dedddeee." For hours, I hugged her and held her hand.

"I love you Tonee. I love you."

As Dawn rose, she slept. Her face was older. I put a little liquid morphine into her mouth.

I called Rita. She thanked me for letting her know. She said she would try to stop by in the afternoon. I called Sandy, her stepsister, in Pennsylvania. I left voice mail that was crying. I called a little later. Sandy answered. She cried and asked to speak to Tonee. I told her Tonee wouldn't speak much and was hard to understand.

I put the phone to Tonee's ear and told her it was Sandy. Her eyes lit. She talked a little, but mostly just listened as Sandy poured love and tears through the phone.

"shussh...shssssh." Tonee was trying to console her.

I spoke to Sandy for a moment. She asked if she could call tomorrow. I apologized for not calling her sooner.

Rita came over in the late afternoon with a big danish pastry in a box. Tonee's huge smile and call welcomed her.

"Rita."

Rita sat next to Tonee and talked to her for a little while.

"I guess this old body of yours has been beat up enough for one lifetime girl. I'm sure you will find a new and a more peaceful place."

Rita kissed her on the lips. She said she'd be back in a couple of days and they'd have a real good girl talk.

An hour later, Rita phoned me and said she didn't want to talk in front of Tonee. The way she was breathing, Rita didn't think she'd be alive in two days. I thanked her for calling. Her call scared the shit out of me. I didn't think I was losing her so quickly.

After the sun went down, Tonee called me to her.

"Bobbie, please don't leave my side tonight. Hold my hand."

"I'm here Tonee. I have your hand. I love you."

"Bobbie, what are you thinking?"

"That this might be our last night together. I love you so much."

"SSSHHH...SShhush. Okay Bobbie?"

Tonee slept most of the night. I held her hand and told her how much I loved her, how I would always love her. Her face was so young and beautiful. She almost had a smile. In the morning, I kissed her awake.

"I love you Bobbie."

The temp nurse came in the morning and at night. Sandy called a couple of more times and talked to Tonee. Tonee barely said anything. She just lit up a little with the voice.

I was scared to death I was spending my last moments with Tonee alive. She had a rough night, squirming and calling out. Mostly, she was quiet and by morning she had fallen asleep. I held her hand all through these precious days and nights.

Francesca, our massage therapist and friend, came over before noon to be with Tonee. Tonee's head lay sideways on the pillow. Her breathing was steady, but she hadn't woke up. Francesca rubbed her head. Tonee's eyes opened, but she didn't respond more.

Joanne's assistant nurse came in the afternoon and called Joanne to come over. Tonee's condition had changed.

He and Joanne gave Tonee a good bath. Her body was leaking from both arms and her right leg. I threw out those sheets and towels. The sores on her back had blistered. Tonee seemed to enjoy the cleaning, but did not talk. Joanne explained to me that Tonee had entered her transition.

Her body and mind were in the zone of change from life to death. Her breathing would be slower. The oxygen would not be needed anymore. This period of life to death was usually a day or two.

Tonee looked beautiful lying there almost unresponsive.

I called Linda and Ken and Lynette and the Rabbi and told them it was time to say goodbye. I called Sandy and she bawled and bawled. She called back a little later and said goodbye to Tonee.

Rita came over and said some beautiful words and kissed her girl goodbye.

The Rabbi was over when Linda came. The Rabbi prayed and talked about the soul and life and death and memories.

Linda spoke loudly as was her strong nature. She talked about the time they met and the talks they had about books and the soul. Linda had always wondered, but never believed in the life and the transition of the soul. Tonee was adamant of her prior lives and the futures to come. She spoke of Tonee's kind and generous nature, of her simple beauty. She spoke of the love she had for her husband. She admired the spunk and the spirit with which she went through her ordeals so many times in the hospital and how she would rebound each time with an energy from God.

"Goodbye Tonee. I love you. It's okay for you to let go." Linda sat down and cried and cried. Then she kissed Tonee on her forehead and left.

I expected Tonee to die that night as I had the night before. I held her hand and talked to her all night.

"I love you Tonee. I will always love you. Don't you ever forget that. I love you Baby girl. It's okay to let go my beautiful wife."

I fed her half doses of liquid morphine hourly. I had always been amazed at how youthful she could look.

In my limited capacity to do so, I prayed for her soul and peace. She'd lived a life with such an inborn sensitive nature that just kept getting beat on. Through all her years, she could still be her three year old or her six year old or her sixteen year old blossoming beauty with the capabilities of an amazon. Her angers were defensive. She had one beautiful voice I called Marilyn because it had that breathless, hurting quality. She was strong and allowed herself love when she had been beaten down so many times in the past. Her gentleness and ability to create beauty from piles of pain amazed me.

I kissed Tonee on her lips. They were still warm and soft. I kissed her eyes and her cheeks and her hand. I couldn't understand why she was put through what she was. I will always admire her love of life.

The Chaplain came over in the afternoon and prayed for the gentle transition to God. She admired the strength she saw in Tonee. She was surprised by the beauty and grace she still held. She said so many deaths did not transition without a face and body twisted and tortured by pain. She kissed Tonee on her forehead and said goodbye. She asked me if there was anything I needed. I thanked her for her care and spirit.

Kona stayed close by confused by what was happening to his Mommy.

Tonee slept quietly through the night. Joanne had told me she didn't need much pain medicine. I held her hand and wiped her nose and lips as she drew longer breaths. I feared sleep for missing her passing moment. In the morning, I was worn, but so happy to breathe again next to my woman.

Joanne came over with her assistant and changed the sheets and gave Tonee a final bath. Her body had passed a large amount of fluids through her arms and legs. Her insides expelled their remaining waste. I threw out all the linens.

As they were bathing Tonee, she almost sat up smiling. A cooing, purring sound I had never heard before came from her lips. She was like a tiny child with the simplest of joys.

Joanne said this was part of the transition into a fetal quality and nature.

They dressed Tonee in a nice blue shirt and lay her back down, covered by the sheet.

Joanne said Tonee had the stamina of a lion. She reminded me to call for a nurse to come for time of death. I admired these people and their love and care on a day to day basis. I thanked them for all their help.

I called Sandy and told her once again it was time to say goodbye.

The Rabbi called a few hours later to check on Tonee. I told him she was passing. He rushed over to say prayers. I thanked him for his care and kindness and spirituality.

I lit Shabbos candles that night. I held Tonee's hand and kept telling her "I love you." All night, I wiped the shmotz from her nose and mouth. I lay back a little trying to rest, holding her warm hand. Her breathing grew harder and slower, sometimes hesitating to start again. As the morning light grew, I kissed her on her forehead. I stood up for a moment and walked around the room. As I was sitting down, I heard a gasp. Her head rose and her blue eyes lit open. She threw her last breath to the air and died. Her right eye was still open. I held her eyelid down till it stayed. Tonee had greeted her last morning sun. It was 7:30.

My time to cry.

Tonee's ashes lie near her Father's in Valhalla, New York. As we near the anniversary of her dying, I hope the healing continues.

She is within me. There is no forgetting my Tonee. I feel her presence, her voices echoing in my memories. I am such a better person for knowing her.

I returned to work a week after her death, but could not function, so I left. My time off led to a writing of the Tonee I know, pen to paper before time's special healing dissipated too many memories. The process was a purging of pain and a healing, cathartic cry.

She is my hero, my lover, my friend, my confidant, my child. The great pride she carried through life; her beautiful body sure in posture, athletic, intelligent, creative, kind, protective.

I doubt many ever knew the multiple girls she carried within her. She found a way to protect her three year old and her six year old and the children thereafter. Why such a creative reaction to childhood pain and futility, I do not know. Tonee lived and worked a good, hard life. Her belief in the soul showed in the way she lived and struggled and played and died.

The suddenness of her cancer and its immediate race to death was shocking. Tonee handled herself with stunning self control. She was kind and caring, asking only for love and enough pain control to keep her from screaming out the insults to her body and mind. She held a simple dignity as was her nature.

I often wonder how she lay the little girls to a final night night. I worry for the little girls.

To the end, she was loving and caring and beautiful. As she slept in her deathbed, her face found youth in dreams. She called for Daddy till she could no longer. Still, she held her beauty and grace.

Each Friday at sunset, I light the Shabbos candles, light flickering on her photo surrounded by amethyst crystals and a bronze angel with fluted glass wings.

"Good Shabbos Tonee. I love you Baby. Find peace."

Kona knows when I grab the leash; he jumps and rushes to the door. The dropping sun shoots orange arrows through the Pali Pass of the nearby Koolau Mountains. I can feel the energy of a near full moon rising as we walk the quiet streets. Plumeria blossoms sweeten the cooling air. Kona stops to sniff, then pushes on tugging at the leash. He knows the way.

"Wowzers Bobbie, I worry bout you."

I imagine the loving voice of my wife looking after me. I worry about the steps she must be taking to find her peace. What a special soul, carrying so much presence, so many voices, so much old memory.

I promised Tonee I would take care of the dog, her son. Thank God for the dog. His simple heart is so full of love and energy; my friend, my companion. With the door shut to the world and the tv on, he's heard my endless cries. How would I have passed these days of loneliness and pain without his company, his love? I can only hope to give him half the massive love Tonee did.

My desire is to bring honor to the life Tonee lived. I am so proud of her. I am so glad to have known her. The days she lived on Earth in this body were never easy. She struggled throughout, but still found love after so many years alone. Her great idea was to protect that little three year old. God bless the children and all the voices within her.

Well, Baby, this lonely year has passed with no epiphany, no gentle tap on my shoulder
"I'm here Bobbie," simply the rich flow of love and memories.

You are within me. Candles flicker as I enjoy wine with your very favorite carrot cake. I thank you for the joy you have shown and given me.

Tonee, Love, it is time for me to say goodbye; for you to let me go.

Robert Becker

www.ingramcontent.com/pod-product-compliance
Lightning Source LLC
Chambersburg PA
CBHW062207280526
45788CB00001B/478